WRESTLECRAP
The Very Worst of Pro Wrestling

R.D. Reynolds

with

Randy Baer

ECW PRESS
ecwpress.com

Copyright © ECW PRESS, 2003

Published by ECW PRESS
2120 Queen Street East, Suite 200, Toronto, Ontario, Canada M4E 1E2

NATIONAL LIBRARY OF CANADA CATALOGUING IN PUBLICATION DATA

Reynolds, R.D., 1969-
WrestleCrap: the very worst of professional wrestling/R.D. Reynolds with Randy Baer.
ISBN 1-55022-584-7
1. Wrestling—Miscellanea. I. Baer, Randy II. Title.
GV1195.R49 2003   796.812   C2003-902188-2

Acquisition and production: Emma McKay, Copy editor: Kevin Flynn
Text design and typesetting: Guylaine Régimbald—Solo Design
Cover design: Jon Heilman, Printing: Transcontinental
Front cover photos: Kiss Demon (top left) and Papa Shango (bottom right) by John Lawson;
Giant Gonzalez (top right) and Double Doink (bottom left) by Jeff Cohen
Back cover photos: Dink and Doink by John Lawson; The Narcissist by Jeff Cohen

This book is set in Cronos

The publication of *WrestleCrap* has been generously supported by the Canada Council, by the Government of Ontario through the Ontario Media Development Corporation's Ontario Book Initiative, by the Ontario Arts Council, and by the Government of Canada through the Book Publising Industry Development Program. Canada

DISTRIBUTION

CANADA: Jaguar Book Group, 100 Armstrong Avenue, Georgetown, Ontario L7G 5S4

UNITED STATES: Independent Publishers Group, 814 North Franklin Street, Chicago, Illinois 60610

EUROPE: Turnaround Publisher Services, Unit 3, Olympia Trading Estate, Coburg Road, Wood Green, London N2Z 6T2

AUSTRALIA AND NEW ZEALAND: Wakefield Press, 1 The Parade West (Box 2266), Kent Town, South Australia 5071

PRINTED AND BOUND IN CANADA

ECW PRESS
ecwpress.com

Dedicated to the memory of my good friend, Merle Vincent Griggs

**I would like to thank the following people
for making this book a reality:**

John Tenta	Kevin Flynn
Eric Kuehling	Troy Ferguson
Casey Stephon	Blade Braxton
Dan Garza	Daniel "M2K" Frantz
Jeff Cohen	Larry "Tiptonium" Tipton
Jon Heilman	Rick Scaia
Anna Poltorak	Scott Keith
Alfonzo Tyson	Bryan Alvarez
Madison Carter	Miss Galatea
Wild Bill Brown	Jason H. Smith
Greg Oliver	Mark Manford
John Lawson	Andre J. Beaucage

Terry and Sally Corman, as well as everyone at Firehouse
Image Center

Xavier Doom's Slayground

Greg Ogorek at GlobalInternet.net

Emma McKay and everyone at ECW Press

Loyal WrestleCrappers everywhere

And most of all, to my wife and family, for putting up
with my wrestling obsession

Special thanks to God above, for helping me to get
through watching all this junk

Contents

Foreword
by John Tenta

My name is John Tenta. It's a name that's familiar to some people in the world of professional wrestling, but unfamiliar to some others. Here in Japan, I am known as John Tenta, or as Koto Tenzan, my former name in professional sumo wrestling But most of you likely know me by my former WWF or WCW ring names: Earthquake, Avalanche, Shark, and Golga the Human Oddity.

I am sitting in a dressing room in Korakoen Hall in Tokyo, Japan. This building has a rich history of pro wrestling, hosting matches anywhere from two to six times a month. Literally thousands of wrestlers have passed through this venue during their careers; others have only dreamed of it. Countless legends of wrestling have competed here, like Giant Baba, Antonio Inoki, Jumbo Tsuruta, Bruiser Brody, Stan Hansen, Abdullah the Butcher, the Funks, Harley Race, and Ric Flair. The list goes on and on and on.

But I am not here to talk about past wrestling champions. No, I'm here to introduce you to a friend of mine, R.D. Reynolds. R.D. has taken the time and effort to compile some of the worst characters and story lines in the history of professional wrestling in the book you now hold in your hands.

So why have I been talking about Japan? Well, it's because it was in this very building, some fifteen years ago, that a boy's dream came true.

My dream. It is here that, at the age of 24, I had my debut match as a professional wrestler, something I had dreamed of since I was six years old.

Mine is just one story of dreams that have come true for thousands of wrestlers. I remember dreaming as a boy that I would one day be a world champion. And although that wish never became a reality, I take pride in the fact that I was one half of the WWF Tag Team Champions known as the Natural Disasters, along with my good friend Typhoon. I am also proud of the fact that I wrestled against world champions such as "Macho Man" Randy Savage, the Ultimate Warrior, and Sting, and, in the highlight of my career, against Hulk Hogan at *SummerSlam*. There I was, in the main event of one of the biggest shows of the year with one of the biggest stars in the history of the business. It is something I will never forget.

I'll never forget being the Shark, either, but not for the same reasons. No one knows for certain whether a wrestler's gimmick will work or fall flat on its face. It's the fans who decide. All that we can do, as wrestlers, is give it our best shot. I didn't like dressing up as a shark, but it was what I was given to do, and I did my best. Some fans even had some fun with it. When fans come up to me now, they inevitably recite an interview I did at the end of the gimmick. "I'm not a shark," I said on *Nitro*. "I'm a man. I'm John Tenta." People remember that, so I guess I did my job.

I actually enjoyed being an Oddity, although I shouldn't have. After all, I was under a mask, so people couldn't even see my face. It really felt like Vince McMahon was punishing me for having deserted the WWF for WCW three years earlier. I still had fun with it, though. I laughed as I danced with the rest of the Oddities, and the fans would dance along. It didn't matter whether we won or lost; we'd dance anyway. It was a short run, but it was a lot of fun.

Being the Shark and being an Oddity — that was WrestleCrap, no doubt about it. But it was also kind of funny. Unlike some folks in this business, I can laugh at it, because I can laugh at myself.

I can also laugh at my friends. Who can forget my former partner Typhoon as the Shockmaster in WCW? I know he wishes that he could.

John Tenta back before they made him a shark, and his partner Typhoon before they obscured his vision with a stormtrooper helmet and shoved him through a wall.

He was actually set for a huge push, but maybe the push was a little *too* big; during his first big entrance he stumbled through a hole in a wall that he'd just burst through. What was that I was saying about some gimmicks falling flat on their faces? Maybe his head, which was covered in a storm-trooper helmet, was getting too big?

Just kidding, Typh — you know I love you.

Hell, Typhoon was the best partner anyone could hope for. He's a true friend, with a heart as big as his huge frame. I knew that if we ever got into trouble, in or out of the ring, he'd be there for me. He's a great man and a great friend, and I still don't believe he knows just how strong he really is. And there's something that unites the two of us in an unbreakable bond: we've both been saddled with WrestleCrap.

I guess that there have been and continue to be bad gimmicks that simply don't work, just as there will always be bad gimmicks that actually get over for some reason or other. I remember Vince McMahon once saying that he could make a star out of anyone. I can't argue that point. He took two WCW outcasts and made them two of the biggest names ever in wrestling: "Stone Cold" Steve Austin and Triple H. Their potential was never realized in WCW, because Eric Bischoff, who ran the promotion, depended on proven stars. Bischoff never gave new guys a chance to succeed. He never knew how to create stars. In fact, I believe that if it hadn't been for the WWF, and the stars that Vince McMahon made who left for WCW, there never would have been a ratings war between *Nitro* and *Raw*. So where's Bischoff now? And where's WCW?

Vince McMahon owns them both.

It's all in the presentation, and it's up to the wrestlers to do their best with what they're given. Austin's and Hunter Hearst Helmsley's initial stints in the WWF weren't anything to write home about, but both they and Vince stuck with it until they achieved success. Hunter could have given up on his original gimmick as a snotty blueblood. He didn't. Austin could have floundered as the Ringmaster, but he just kept trying. And Vince gave them both the chance to succeed.

I too have had my share of lame gimmicks, but I hold my head high. I did the best I could with what I was given, and, fortunately, I have never had to do anything that would embarrass my wife or my family. Remember when I squashed Jake Roberts's pet snake, Damien? And made snakeburgers out of him? Was that WrestleCrap? You're darn right it was, but it was funny.

Some people hated me for that. Great! That's just what I was going for. They hated me in my WWF debut when I came out of the audience and squashed the Ultimate Warrior. They hated me when I put Hulk Hogan out of the WWF. They hated me when I killed Jake's snake. They hated me when I destroyed Andre the Giant's knee, putting him out of the WWF. And they hated me when I turned Tugboat into Typhoon.

Now ask yourself this: did I make the people hate me, or did Vince McMahon and his matchmakers do it? Vince was the director, and I filled the role. It made me a star. Earthquake became a hated name. That is what we wrestlers do; whether good or bad, we try our best to succeed at the roles we are given. For every Stone Cold, there are a hundred Sharks.

But underneath the gimmicks, wrestlers are all just men and women trying hard to be successful in their jobs. We're trying to climb that ladder to the top, even though the ladder may have a few rungs missing or be a little short. We do what is asked of us. Sometimes people ask me why I agreed to play the role of a fish man. The answer is plain and simple: if I hadn't, there were plenty of other people who would have. I just wanted to be able to provide for my family. I was just a guy trying to make a living. Take away my gimmicks, good and bad, and I'm a regular person just like you.

With that in mind, it is with pleasure that I now hand the reins of this book over to its author and a true lover of pro wrestling: R.D. Reynolds. I hope that you'll find yourself smiling and laughing out loud as much as I did while you read.

And now, as I leave this wrestling hall in Tokyo, where it all started for me, I reflect upon my career. I have no false hopes or new dreams that

I will ever return to WWE, but I do find comfort—and considerable joy—in the fact that I made memories for myself and for others. And I thank God for letting this boy's dream come true.

Enjoy this book, and enjoy pro wrestling.

And always remember: crap happens.

Stand Back!
That Egg Is Ready to Blow!

It was Thanksgiving Night, and fans were pouring into the Hartford Civic Arena. Some had driven for hours, trading turkey dinner with Grandma for some slop at a roadside greasy spoon, just to be there. After all, they had been waiting for months for this one. There was no way they would pass up this opportunity.

The event was *Survivor Series*, one of the four biggest shows the World Wrestling Federation would present all year.

There were fans of the immortal Hulk Hogan, longing to see their hero tangle with the vile Earthquake. Others came to watch Jake Roberts get his hands on "The Model" Rick Martel, who had blinded Jake weeks earlier. And then there were those who came solely to witness the Ultimate Warrior run down the aisle and obliterate every opponent in sight.

While each fan had his or her own favorite wrestler, everyone was excited about one thing. Tonight was the night, finally, that they would get to see what was inside that egg.

Yes, the egg. But this wasn't just any old giant egg. This was a mysterious giant egg. For months the WWF had carted the egg around to every arena it visited, and announcers had hyped that it would hatch on Thanksgiving Night. No one in the audience knew what significance the egg actually had. After all, what the heck did an egg have to do with pro wrestling? Whatever it was, it must have been important, or the WWF wouldn't have spent so much time hyping it. What could be inside that giant egg?

While the promotion was keeping its lips sealed, fans had their own ideas. Maybe it would be a new wrestler making his debut. Perhaps a bodybuilder, signifying the launch of the WWF's new sister company, the World Bodybuilding Federation. Could it be a celebrity of some sort? After all, the promotion had used everyone from Liberace to Bob Uecker to drum up attention in the past.

Whatever it was, there were only two ways those fans would be able to find out: be there live and in person, or cough up the $24.95 to watch it on cable.

Over 10,000 fans showed up in Hartford on that fateful evening, with hundreds of thousands more watching from the comfort of their own homes. Throughout the night, various shots of the egg were shown as the matches took place. Speculation was running rampant. What the hell could it be?

Finally, the moment of truth arrived. Announcers Gorilla Monsoon and Roddy Piper handed the telecast over to "Mean Gene" Okerlund, who was eggside. "This cracks me up," Okerlund lamely joked, as he hyped one last time what might be inside the egg. Could it be a dinosaur? Balloons? Maybe the Playmate of the Month?

Finally, the moment everyone had waited for had arrived.

"Stand back! Stand back! That egg is ready to blow!"

Out from the egg it came!

It was . . . it was . . . a *turkey*?

A guy dressed up as a *turkey*?

Fans sat in stunned silence as Okerlund continued a hype job worthy of P.T. Barnum. "Take a look at him, ladies and gentlemen! He's got feathers, a beak, and a little rooster tail up on top! Look at the feet on this thing!"

The bird hopped down to Okerlund.

It spoke: "Gobbledy gobbledy!!"

Okerlund looked amazed. "What's with the gobbledy?"

"Gobbledy gobbledy!" it replied.

"Gobbledy gobbledy?" Okerlund asked. "Don't tell me you're the Gobbledy Gooker!"

The feathered man nodded excitedly, his Wiffle ball eyes nearly falling off his costumed head.

Suddenly, a rock & roll version of "Turkey in the Straw" began to blare over the loudspeakers. The feathered creature dragged Okerlund to the ring as the TV commentators wondered aloud what was going to happen next. The bird hopped over the top rope and motioned for Mean Gene to follow. Reluctantly, Okerlund entered the ring. A smattering of boos began to emanate from the crowd, but that fact seemed lost on Piper. "The kids are going nuts!" he exclaimed. "They love him!" Meanwhile, a teenager in the crowd flipped the bird the bird.

The Gooker began to flap his arms and shuffle about. He hooked Okerlund's arm and the two performed the world's most bizarre square dance. Gene did the best jig his fifty-something-year-old body could manage, as the turkey man started bouncing off the ropes, his journey culminating in a backflip. He motioned for Okerlund to do the same. Gene ran from rope to rope, then fell flat on his face.

The scattered boos grew to a mammoth roar of disapproval as the skit entered its seventh minute.

"They didn't know what to make of him at first, but I think he's won the heart of Hartford!" Piper theorized.

"He sure has!" Monsoon agreed. "Gobbledy Gooker, a big smash here at *Survivor Series!*"

The boos became deafening as the Gooker left the arena, thousands of voices joining together to let the WWF know how much they hated what they had just seen. For those fans, both in the arena and at home, had just been forced to endure ten minutes of WrestleCrap.

•   •   •

Professional wrestling is a huge business. According to its fourth-quarter fiscal report, the World Wrestling Federation grossed $456 million in 2001.

As impressive as that amount might be, it is also an important reminder that pro wrestling is a business. Period. It isn't an athletic contest, nor is it about entertaining fans. It is all about one thing, and that's making money. Please keep this in mind as you read this book. Because as hard as it may be to believe, all the events, all the characters, everything presented here actually happened. What's even more unbelievable is that it all happened because someone, for God knows what reason, thought it would make money. Yes, someone, somewhere, actually believed that the Gobbeldy Gooker would make fans at home open up their wallets and head to the arenas.

It isn't my intention to mock those who have portrayed the characters or performed in the skits that I describe in this book. The fact of the matter is, I'm a lifelong wrestling fan, and the last thing I want to do is ridicule the men and women who have been asked to perform some of the ridiculous antics presented to them by the writers. In fact, these wrestlers likely had little say in the matter. Refusal to do as they'd been told would have been rewarded with a trip to the unemployment office.

The people that came up with the ideas, though, are fair game.

And who exactly is that? In wrestling, this person is known as the *booker*. Sometimes, if more than one person is involved, they are given other titles, such as the *creative department* or the *booking team*. It is their duty to create *gimmicks*, or characters, for the wrestlers. They are also in charge of writing *angles*, or story lines, that perpetuate rivalries, or *feuds*, between the wrestlers.

Within the wrestling community, the men and women who slam one another to the mat in the ring aren't called "wrestlers" at all; they're *workers*. Like your average Joe Sixpack at a construction site, if a guy wrestles hard and is entertaining, he is known as a "good worker." Conversely, a guy who mails it in and puts fans to sleep is known as a "bad worker."

Workers are traditionally defined by their moral alignment. A good guy in wrestling is known as a *babyface*, or *face* for short. The bad guy who attacks his opponent before the opening bell and laughs in a manner most vile? That would be the *heel*. A good face can make the crowd *pop*, or react positively to his antics in the ring. A good heel can generate *heat*, which means that the fans will boo every move he makes, and they will get into his match every bit as much as they do for the most popular of faces. If a heel is good enough at getting heat, then fans, or *marks*, will pay to see him get his comeuppance.

The goal of any wrestling company, as I've already pointed out, is to make money. Wrestling companies, or *promotions*, do this in various ways, but all of them involve convincing fans to sink time and money into their product. It is therefore the responsibility of the company to convince fans to buy tickets to events, watch TV shows, and buy pay-per-view events; hence the term *promotion*. First the company promotes the event itself, convincing fans to buy tickets to the show. Then, once they're in the door, these fans will also purchase merchandise, such as T-shirts and hats, that will fatten the company's (and often the performers') pocketbooks. This happens every night in cities across North America, where wrestling promotions large and small present nontelevised live events.

But you don't have to be at a live event to add your money to a promotion's coffers. Pay-per-views (PPVs for short) are special events that fans pay their local cable company to watch. The higher the *buy rate*, the more money the wrestling promotion makes. These are generally the biggest moneymakers a national promotion has; it is not inconceivable for a wrestling company to make several million dollars in one night by promoting a PPV event. Pay-per-view events are doubly lucrative; the promotion takes in revenue not only from the cable buys, but also from the increased seat sales possible at such events, which are generally presented in larger arenas, often with capacity crowds. *Wrestlemania III*, for example, took place in the Pontiac Silverdome before a crowd of 78,000 fans. (A number the WWF inflated to 93,000 because they believed that 78,000 wasn't impressive enough. Welcome to the hyperbole-driven world of pro wrestling.) Add in the cable buys and any merchandise fans may have bought, and it's easy to see why it is of utmost importance that these events be promoted well.

Of course, there are always the various regular wrestling programs on television as well. Just like any other television show, they are deemed a success or failure based on their ratings. The more people who watch the show, the more the television network can charge companies for the advertising time they buy. When ratings are high, wrestling companies make a lot of money. When ratings are low, however, they face the same issues other shows face, such as low advertising rates or cancellation. It may be wrestling, but to the networks, it's more or less the same as any other program they air. So, in order to thrive—and even to survive—wrestling promotions have to do everything they can to attract fans and hold on to them.

Often, in the quest to create something wrestling fans want to see, the promotion will make a serious error in judgment. When this happens, whether it be in the form of a character fans find ridiculous or a story line that has more holes than Swiss cheese, a promotion has created what I refer to as "WrestleCrap."

WrestleCrap has quite literally destroyed men's lives. It has caused gigantic, multimillion-dollar companies to perish. But more than anything, it has caused millions of innocent viewers to shake their heads and wonder, "Who in the hell thought *this* was a good idea?"

If you are a wrestling fan, this book will likely remind you of characters that that you thought—or hoped—were just a bad dream. And for those of you who know nothing about the wrestling business, don't fret.

After all, stupidity is a universal language.

The Circus Comes to Town

Despite what many of its detractors might have you believe, the World Wrestling Federation did not invent WrestleCrap. Bizarre characters and story lines have been prevalent since the early days of the business.

It wasn't until the advent of television, however, that the first wildly successful "gimmick" came to be. As the medium began to gain public acceptance in the 1950s, networks were in need of cheap programming. Pro wrestling fit the bill, with the added bonus of drawing generally high ratings. It was a match made in heaven.

About this time, a thirty-five-year-old man by the name of George Wagner appeared on the scene. Unlike other wrestlers of the era, who would come to the ring wearing black tights and boots, Wagner would appear wearing long, flowing robes and curlers in his bleached blond hair. His demeanor was most peculiar; he was as prissy as humanly possible. Before he would even think about entering the ring, he would instruct his valet to spray the area with perfume. After all, the last thing he wanted was to reek like his opponent.

He was dubbed "Gorgeous" George by announcers, and he is generally regarded as the first man in pro wrestling history to play up showmanship over athleticism. Fans ate it up—they couldn't wait to see this pantywaist get clobbered. George, playing the heel, would use every illegal tactic he could to defeat his opponents. The more he cheated, the more people hated him. And the more people hated him, the more they were willing to tune in to see him get what was coming to him.

Although Gorgeous George's gimmick was a success, other ideas weren't quite so well received. Wrestlers were given all manner of oddball personas in hopes that the public would take notice. There were characters based on superheroes, such as Batman. During the late 1960s, a mop-topped wrestler named George Ringo, dubbed the "Wrestling Beatle," would carry a guitar to the ring. Frankensteins, vampires, and werewolves all cavorted about in the ring. There were even various wrestling mummies, wrapped from head to toe in bandages. One of the mummies, in an effort to prove his authenticity, cut his finger in half, causing sand to pour out.

Still, these characters were the exception, not the rule. Most wrestlers continued to compete in standard trunks, allowing their skills inside the squared circle to be their calling card. Men such as Harley Race and Jack Brisco thrilled crowds with their technical prowess, not by dressing up as movie monsters.

These men performed in regional territories throughout the United States. Prior to the early 1980s, there were imaginary boundaries that promoters did not dare cross. Verne Gagne and his American Wrestling Association (AWA) handled the Midwest, specifically the Minneapolis region. The National Wrestling Alliance (NWA) handled the Atlantic seaboard, running huge shows at the Omni in Atlanta on a regular basis. And Vince McMahon Sr.'s World Wide Wrestling Federation (WWWF) controlled the Northeast, including the crown jewel of all arenas, Madison Square Garden in New York City.

Vincent J. McMahon adhered to the territorial guidelines. He did not run shows in Atlanta, nor did he venture to the Midwest. He did not attempt to hire performers away from other promotions. He believed that there was enough of the wrestling pie for all promoters to gorge themselves on.

Vincent K. McMahon, on the other hand, did not share his father's beliefs. After purchasing the WWWF from his dad and dropping the "Wide" from its name, the younger McMahon had but one thought in mind: to conquer all in his path and create a North American pro wrestling monopoly. He completely ignored the territorial boundaries and ran shows throughout the United States. He also threw boatloads of money at each area's top stars, which bolstered his roster while effectively killing off the rival promotion.

As Vince McMahon examined his roster, he came to the realization that his world champion, a former collegiate wrestling star by the name of Bob Backlund, was too bland to shake things up to the degree necessary to turn the WWF into a national phenomenon. McMahon needed someone who was larger than life. He needed Hulk Hogan.

Hogan, born Terry Bollea, was everything that Backlund wasn't. Backlund made a name for himself in the collegiate wrestling ranks. Hogan made a name for himself starring in *Rocky III*, opposite Sylvester Stallone. Whereas Backlund was quiet and soft-spoken, Hogan was loud and boisterous. Backlund worked over his opponents with a mat-based attack. Hogan destroyed his opponents with fists and clotheslines. The fact that Hogan couldn't wrestle a lick didn't really matter. The success of Vince's promotion wouldn't be based on the wrestling ability of its workers. Instead, he would rely on a story-driven formula that required the creation and manipulation of all sorts of outrageous characters.

Although McMahon would claim in later years that his predecessors only ran wrestling shows in "smoky bars and bingo parlors," this was not the case. Pro wrestling regularly sold out such venues as Madison Square Garden long before Hulk Hogan took to the national stage. It is true, however, that Vince was able to sell the public on the fact that his product was something the whole family could enjoy, and he began to create a target market based on the preteen demographic.

In order to do this, he made his workers more than just wrestlers. In fact, they were no longer even referred to as "wrestlers." No, his men were "superstars." He wanted his personnel to be more akin to superheroes than the ugly marauders that had been the staple of pro wrestling since its origins. To that end, Hogan's initial name was the "Incredible Hulk" Hogan, borrowed, of course, from a popular Marvel Comics superhero. The WWF had to pay to use the trademarked name, which Vince grudgingly did in order to perpetuate the image that Hogan was more than just a mere mortal wrestler.

With his syndicated television show being aired primarily on Saturday mornings, Vince decided to keep the characters as basic as possible, so that kids could follow along. McMahon's wrestlers — that is, superstars — were no longer identified by what they did in the ring, but rather by what their personas did outside it. The WWF presented cartoonish, larger-than-life characters, the thought being that this would appeal to the preteen set. This infuriated hardcore wrestling fans, who began calling the WWF a circus and an insult to the sport they held dear.

McMahon didn't care. It wasn't a sport, anyway. It wasn't wrestling. It was "sports entertainment" — a term manufactured by McMahon and his cronies so that their business wouldn't be regulated as pro wrestling had been in the past.

Vince made his views clear in a 1986 interview with Larry King. When asked if he could be considered the Don King of wrestling, he replied, "No, I am the Walt Disney of wrestling."

McMahon's goal was to steer his wrestling company sharply away from its identity as a "sport" and into the spotlights and big bucks of showbiz. Let them call it a circus. It still featured just enough wrestling that the old-school fans would continue to attend the matches. And if they didn't, who cared? His audience was, by now, much broader than the relatively small number of marks who bought the magazines and debated over who had the best figure four leglock.

In order to play to this broader audience, McMahon created charac-ters who were simple, generally based upon tried and true stereotypes. For ex-ample, the WWF employed no less than four different hillbillies. First came Hillbilly Jim, from Mudlick, Kentucky. According to the story line, Jim was just a friendly bumpkin who ran in from the crowd one night to save his fav-o-rite 'rassler, Hulk Hogan, from a postmatch beating. To repay him for saving his hide, Hogan trained Jim to become a grappler himself. During a series of televised skits, Jim learned the ropes through such state-of-the-art training methods as bear-hugging an old tire, dropping knees on a stained mattress, and wrestling his coon dog. In the background, his granny drank moonshine from a jug. Wheeeeeee doggies! Now that there's enter-tainment!

Like an unwanted litter of pups, the hillbilly kin just kept on a-growin', as Cousin Luke and Cousin Junior both entered the fray to defend the honor of slack-jawed yokels throughout the confederacy. Deciding that three hillbillies just weren't enough, Vince imported Stan Frazier as Jim's 400-pound Uncle Elmer. How did this hillbilly get so fat? By partaking in a bucket of "Uncle Elmer's Fried Pig Parts," of course.

Apparently, the ability to eat inordinate amounts of deep-fried sow slop was enough to make impressionable young women swoon, as Elmer soon found himself a lady friend. After a brief courtship, the two married in a televised ceremony. The event was presented on NBC television and was attended by no less a celebrity than Tiny Tim. Yes, "Tiptoe Through the Tulips" Tiny Tim.

It didn't matter to McMahon that Tiny Tim's only claim to fame was a fifteen-year-old novelty song featuring his warbling voice and equally

Break out the moonshine, Granny!
It's a good ol'-fashion hillbilly wedding! Wheeeeeee doggies!

annoying ukulele. You see, he too had been married on TV, on the *Tonight Show*, although it is likely no one in the audience remembered that fact. What mattered to Vince McMahon was that Tim had been, at some point in life, famous. McMahon had used this very philosophy when presenting the very first *Wrestlemania* telecast, signing up Muhammad Ali, Billy Martin, Cyndi Lauper, Mr. T, and Liberace to take part in the event. It didn't matter that these stars had nothing at all to do with wrestling; what mattered was that some of their showbiz fame might—just might—rub off on the WWF.

If hillbillies were the WWF's fan favorites, foreigners made up Vince's rogues' gallery. Chief among the bad-guy brigade was the Iron Sheik, direct from Tehran, Iran. Upon beating his opponent to the mat, the Sheik would twirl his handlebar mustache like a villain from a silent movie. After screaming "Iran number one!" he would proceed to kick his curly-toed boot into the mat three times so as to "load" it with a foreign object of some sort. To this day, it remains a mystery what, exactly, was loaded into the boot, or why the mystical number of kicks was always three. Much like Bigfoot and Stonehenge, this riddle will likely remain forever unsolved.

Sheik's partner in crime was barrel-chested Russian Nikolai Volkoff, who would infuriate crowds by singing the Russkie national anthem. He was later joined by Boris Zukhov, who could not only sing, but also had the added advantage of having the world's largest cranium. It was also almost perfectly round. No kidding—his head resembled one of those old medicine balls they had in gyms in the 1960s.

Despite the long history of evil foreign wrestlers in the WWF, though, there was one babyface from outside the good ol' U.S. of A. Riding the wave of popularity of all things Australian that began with the movie *Crocodile Dundee*, promos hyping the impending arrival of Outback Jack began airing in early 1987. These segments were usually quite lengthy, and they ate up a lot of valuable airtime that could have been used to hype upcoming events or pay-per-views. The sketches were very well produced and provided a fascinating look inside this Aussie's life. Jack dressed as any stereotypical native of the land down under would, complete with outback hat, and if his gap-toothed grin didn't scream "Australia," it's hard to imagine what would. He'd spend time in these promos driving around in his jeep, hanging out with aborigines, and drinking beer with cows. You wouldn't think a bar would let Elsie in, but there she was, downing a Foster's with our new Australian friend.

For all the buildup, however, it appeared that someone forgot that Jack would eventually have to compete inside the ring. Once he began actually wrestling, it became apparent that he had either never done that before or that he had and just really, really sucked. In addition, Jack also laid claim to quite possibly the dumbest finishing move of all time. He would clothesline his opponent from the front, then wait patiently for him to get back up before clobbering him again with a clothesline to the back of the neck. It was called, of course, the boomerang.

Jack's stint in the WWF was very, very brief, as the promotion realized that he simply couldn't cut it as a wrestler. As awful as he was, though, the WWF thought enough of him to craft an officially licensed Outback Jack action figure. These figures are extremely rare and have been known to go for as much as $1.99 on eBay.

The WWF's treatment of foreigners might have played on stereotypes, but its portrayal of blacks bordered on being racist. Tony Atlas, for instance, was down on his luck and looking for work. Atlas was a bodybuilder who had gained a modest level of fame under the monikers "Mr. U.S.A." and "Black Superman" in the pre-*Wrestlemania* WWF. When Hogan came to town, Atlas left McMahon's company and competed in the World Class area. That didn't quite work out, so he came back to McMahon asking for a job. McMahon, possibly bitter that Atlas had left earlier, came up with a most delightful idea for his character: Atlas would become Saba Simba, African Tribesman.

Sounded noble enough, until you saw him head to the ring. Atlas looked anything but dignified as he danced barefoot down the aisle wearing a gigantic feather headdress. The headgear was so large, in fact, that he had a hard time getting through the ropes while wearing it. Once inside the squared circle, Atlas would continue the routine, jumping around like a savage walking on hot coals.

At this point you're probably saying to yourself, "Yeah, that's bad, but it could have been worse. It wasn't like he came out with a spear or anything." Except that he did. In fact, Saba carried not only a spear to the ring, but a large shield as well. Maybe he was afraid of the African Americans in the crowd hurling garbage at him in the ring. During his play-by-play commentary, McMahon claimed that this was a man returning to his roots, which suggests that spears had been an integral part of his development during his early years. Odd. You'd think Roanoke, Virginia, where Tony Atlas was actually from, would have been a little more civilized in the 1960s. The company proceeded to have Atlas humiliate himself and then had the audacity to fire him mere weeks later.

By this point, you're probably thinking to yourself, again, that it still could have been worse. At least they didn't make him out to be a cannibal. And on that count you'd be right. Even Vince and his cronies wouldn't stoop that low.

After all, that had already been done.

His name was Kamala, and he supposedly hailed from deepest, darkest Africa. He was a sight to behold: a huge man, standing about 6'4" and weighing almost 400 pounds, who wore a giant mask to the ring and had stars and moons painted across his face and body. He didn't speak a word, but yelped like a dog in a great deal of pain. He had a handler, Kim Chee, and various managers who spoke with malevolent glee of how Kamala looked forward to boiling his opponent (no doubt garnished with potatoes and carrots) in a giant pot.

Although Kamala didn't begin his gimmick in the WWF, it is there that he gained the most notoriety. Eventually, though, even the WWF came to realize that maybe this wasn't such a great idea after all. He was turned babyface, becoming the world's first fan-friendly cannibal. He was put under the wing of yet another black man, the Reverend Slick, who attempted to "humanize" Kamala. In a scene right out of *The Elephant Man*, Slick preached that Kamala was a man, not an animal, and did his best to teach Kamala the ways of civilized life. This led to a whole slew of skits, including an infamous one in which Kamala learned to bowl. Because God knows that you're just not civilized until you've won a beer frame.

While the good Reverend Slick may have been a legitimate man of the cloth by that point in his career, that wasn't always the case. He too was given a rather questionable identity upon his entrance into the company: the Doctor of Style, a fast-talkin' brother from the hood. His theme song, "Jive Soul Bro," came complete with a video that highlighted his oversized lips and showed him mowing down fried chicken. Shocking that the company didn't have him slurping on a watermelon as well.

During his run as a heel, Slick had another notable protégé. In the late 1980s, the WWF brought in the One Man Gang, a burly man from the mean streets of Chicago. He had been on the wrestling scene for quite some time, having gained notoriety in the old World Class area. His image, with dark sunglasses, a mohawk, and a tattoo on the side of his skull, was one that wrestling fans would always remember. For reasons unknown, however, the WWF felt this character was played out and in need of a makeover.

He got just that during a parking-lot voodoo ceremony overseen by the Slickster. As "natives" danced about carrying spears, a trash can exploded into a ball of flame. When the smoke cleared, the former One Man

Gang emerged in a yellow and blue outfit that made him look like the world's largest Easter egg. Slick presented his charge to the world as Akeem, the African Dream. The manager presented Akeem with his very own boom box as a final rite of passage.

It was just like Saba Simba, with one major exception: George Gray, who portrayed the One Man Gang and Akeem, was *white*. He was truly a sight to behold as he attempted to jive talk with his slight southern accent (Gray was originally from South Carolina). Really made you believe in the character.

Aside from stereotypes, McMahon had some other interesting ways of defining his superstars. Consider "Magnificent" Don Muraco and his manager, Mr. Fuji. They planned to use the WWF to showcase their acting talents and land gigs in Hollywood. The entirely foreseeable irony was that they couldn't act to save their lives.

Fuji (real name, Harry Fujiwara) spoke broken English with a decidedly Japanese accent, while the burly Muraco growled his lines as though he were chewing on marbles. That didn't stop the duo from trying, however, as they set out to conquer every genre imaginable. There was *Fuji Vice*, in which Muraco and Fuji did their best Crockett and Tubbs impersonation; *Fuji General*, a soap opera spoof; *Fuji Chan*, a murder mystery; and *Fuji Bandito*, a spaghetti western starring 60-year-old woman's champ Fabulous Moolah as a cancan girl.

The idea was that the fans who were forced to sit through these skits would hate Fuji and Muraco due to their horrid acting skills. But the segments were so hilarious that the reverse actually happened. Fuji and Muraco had a chemistry that made them almost impossible to hate. At times, the pair resembled the old *Carol Burnett Show* duo of Tim Conway and Harvey Korman, who would do their damnedest to make each other laugh. More than once, Muraco was caught on camera attempting to suppress his chuckling. It's not hard to imagine fans at home doing the same.

The Fuji-Muraco films were usually presented on the WWF's *Tuesday Night Titans* (*TNT*) program. *TNT* was more or less a variety show, with wrestlers singing, dancing, and being interviewed. There was no wrestling featured on the show at all. Loyal viewers were treated, instead, to the superstars of the WWF furthering their characters by performing in nonsensical sketches. Roddy Piper, for example, portrayed Ebenezer Scrooge in a re-enactment of Charles Dickens's *A Christmas Carol*, and he decided that he was better off keeping all his money. The Texan duo known as the Funks had a barbecue and then hung announcer Lord Alfred Hayes from a tree. And the tag team known as the Hart Foundation competed for a date on "The Mating Game," during which manager Jimmy Hart explained that his idea of foreplay was to "take out some baby oil, oil up my megaphone, and stick it right in your ear." It was a showcase of the absurd, and it required the WWF cast to utilize their acting abilities the best they could.

Of course, acting ability, either as a part of an angle or not, was just one part of being a WWF superstar. It was important that the wrestlers looked the part as well. While muscle-bound characters were always popular in wrestling, Vince took the importance of this characteristic to new heights as he imported weight lifters who had never set foot inside a wrestling ring. A perfect example of this was Ted Arcidi, who had the distinction of being known as the World's Strongest Man. For once, this wasn't just some hokey wrestling gimmick; Arcidi was the first man to officially bench-press 700 pounds, a feat he accomplished at the International Hawaiian Powerlifting Championships in 1984.

It should come as no shock that, after this impressive feat, wrestling promoters would come calling. Both the WWF and the NWA actively pursued Arcidi. Sadly, the world was robbed of any potential classics between Arcidi and then-champ Ric Flair, as Arcidi wound up with the WWF in early 1986, while Flair was still with the NWA. And who could question McMahon for shelling out the cash to bring the guy in? Think about it—this guy could lift *seven hundred pounds*! See that Frigidaire in your kitchen? Good. Now tie three of them together and give us a few reps. Arcidi could actually do that.

The only problem, of course, was that Arcidi moved with all the grace of the aforementioned ice box. He was so muscular that even moving about the ring was a chore, and he could only accomplish the most basic of maneuvers. Many consider him one of the worst wrestlers to ever enter the squared circle. He was so bad, in fact, that even the WWF realized that it wasn't going to work out and cut him loose. His only notable match was at the *Wrestlemania II* battle royal, in which Arcidi fell to the floor in short order, despite the cheers of special timekeeper Clare Peller.

What's that you say? You don't remember who Clare Peller was? She was the woman who asked, "Where's the beef?" in a series of commercials for the Wendy's restaurant chain in the mid-'80s. Like Tiny Tim, she was famous, so there may have been potential for her to draw in new viewers. Maybe Vince thought she would bring in the fast food crowd.

It wasn't just Arcidi who was light on wrestling skills; very few of the WWF superstars of the period were what you would call "classic" wrestlers. WWF announcer Gorilla Monsoon would often refer to guys who didn't know "a wrist lock from a wristwatch," and, truth be told, that would have applied to most of the WWF roster. Again, McMahon didn't care—he wanted characters, not wrestlers.

One guy who did know how to wrestle, though, was a gentleman by the name of Keith Franke, known to wrestling fans as Adrian Adonis. Adonis, who had held regional titles all over the country, had been portrayed throughout his career as a street thug from New York City. Although he always had a fair amount of baby fat, he was a hell of a worker, able to perform as well as men half his size. At some point in late 1985, however, Adonis's physique went completely south, and he ballooned to well over 350 pounds. McMahon was extremely displeased, and he decided to send a message to his employees by giving Adonis a gimmick that no wrestler wanted.

Tough-guy biker Adrian Adonis was gone. In his place was "Adorable" Adrian Adonis, the world's first openly gay pro wrestler. The heat for this was incredible, but it was a kind of cheap heat that caused crowds to turn ugly with chants of "Faggot!" and other none-too-kind slurs. For his part, though, Adonis played the character to the hilt. He wore makeup, and bows in his hair. He would give interviews in which he would sing to other wrestlers, including a breathtaking rendition of "Hey Paula," which he sang to Paul Orndorff. It was not uncommon to see him prance out to ringside wearing a dress that would usually get stripped off his bulbous torso to reveal a bra and granny panties underneath.

Adonis began to generate so much interest that he was given his own talk show segment on WWF television, "The Flower Shop." The airtime was open due to the fact that Roddy Piper, who previously did this type of segment with his trailblazing "Piper's Pit," had left the promotion in order to film the science fiction flick *They Live*. Upon Piper's return to the WWF, he immediately began to feud with Adonis, going so far as to destroy the set of "The Flower Shop," setting up a match in which he defeated Adonis. Following this showdown, the Adorable one had his head shaved by Brutus "The Barber" Beefcake, presumably to establish a feud between Adonis and Beefcake. Before the feud ever took place, however, Adonis was fired by the WWF. Various rumors have floated around for years as to the reason for the termination, but the one that's generally accepted as the truth is that Adonis was a slob outside the ring and projected a bad image for the company.

While it was expected that Keith Franke's Adonis persona would get over, there had to have been those within the WWF who thought Wayne Farris didn't have a prayer of being a main eventer. Farris's gimmick was anything but subtle; he was the Honky Tonk Man, an Elvis Presley imper-sonator. Actually, that's not entirely true, since he claimed at every step that he had no idea who "Elvis" was, even though he dressed and acted just like the King. The mere thought of an Elvis-impersonating wrestler has to be one of the most bizarre ideas ever, and Honky Tonk was anything but a technician inside the ropes.

Upon his arrival into the WWF, Honky Tonk was a babyface, with the seal of approval from no less than Hulk Hogan. Despite this, fans hated the guy, booing him upon his entrance to the ring, during his matches, and afterwards as well. And remember: they weren't being told to boo him; they were being told to cheer him. Rather than give up on the Honky Tonk experiment, McMahon went the opposite direction and turned him heel. With this opening, Farris busted his ass and was able to get over by playing everything completely over the top. From his entrance, in which he shim-mied and shaked his way to the ring, to his cheating ways, Honky annoyed fans to no end by mistaking their boos for cheers. His exit from the ring just added fuel to the fire, as he would grab the microphone and exclaim, "Thank you for your support — you're a beautiful audience!" After this, fans were more than willing to pay to see him get clobbered.

Eventually, though, Honky Tonk wore out his welcome and, with nothing better to do, was paired up with an aging Greg "The Hammer"

Valentine. Valentine was a second-generation grappler who had achieved fame in the old NWA territory and during a pair of Intercontinental title reigns in the WWF. He was famous for taking a fall that looked like a tree being chopped over, with his face landing right on the mat. He was built like a fireplug, short and stocky, with bleached blond hair.

In order to form the team Rhythm & Blues, Valentine completely altered his appearance. He dyed his blonde hair jet black—just like Honky Tonk. He would wear Elvis outfits—just like Honky Tonk. He started toting around a guitar—just like Honky Tonk. He was, for lack of a better term, an Elvis impersonator–impersonator.

If the team was meant to be Honky Tonk doubled, it worked, as fans got tired of Honky twice as fast. Valentine looked like a buffoon, with a character that was about as far removed as possible from the one he played through his career. Announcer Gorilla Monsoon labeled Valentine "Boxcar," possibly as a reference to Boxcar Willie, which certainly didn't do much for Valentine's credibility.

McMahon tried everything he could think of to grab fans' attention. There was even a brief period in the late 1980s during which the WWF seemed less a wrestling promotion than a traveling petting zoo. To be fair, animals had been used in pro wrestling prior to this. During the 1960s and early 70s, regional promotions sometimes pitted their workers against bears. Yes, live bears. Hey, who wouldn't pay to see Chief Jay Strongbow tangle with Gentle Ben?

The WWF didn't go quite that far, but what they did was question-able enough. The trend began around 1986 when a lean and lanky Georgian by the name of Jake Roberts entered the company. Roberts had made his name throughout the south, and made a huge impact on the WWF upon his arrival. What Roberts lacked in physical gifts he more than made up for in ring psychology. He had an innate ability to manipulate the fans' emotions to his liking. He could do it not only with his interviews, but also with simple body language. He was truly a master of the subtle art of pro wrestling.

His long, lithe body was almost serpent-like, so he adapted the ring name of Jake "The Snake." McMahon decided that being named after a snake wasn't quite enough, and that Jake should actually bring a snake with him to the ring. So Jake threw a huge python named Damien into a burlap sack and hauled him to the ring for each and every match. After defeating his opponents, he would take the snake out of the bag and allow it to squirm all over his foe's fallen body. Sometimes, he would take its head and put it in the adversary's mouth.

More animals were forthcoming. First came "The Birdman" Koko B. Ware. A veteran of the Memphis wrestling scene, Koko took the animal gimmick to a whole new level. He not only brought a pet macaw named Frankie to the ring with him, but also encouraged fans to flap their arms during his matches. He also sang his own theme song, imploring fans to do the "Bird Bird Bird, do the Bird Bird Bird."

The British Bulldogs were also "blessed" with an animal mascot. The team had pioneered many high-flying tactics in the WWF, and drew the old school wrestling fans to WWF shows. However, injuries to the Dynamite Kid had left him a shell of his former self. McMahon decided that what the duo really needed was to have a live canine escort them to the ring, so they were given a bulldog named Matilda. That went over like a fart in church, and the Bulldogs departed shortly thereafter.

At least Roberts, Ware, and the Bulldogs simply carried animals to the ring. One man was forced to portray one. Terry Taylor was an up-and-coming wrestler for the NWA when he was lured to the WWF with promises of

fame and fortune. Upon entering the company, he was paired with manager Bobby Heenan, who claimed that he could take a guy of average size
with average ability, like Taylor, and, using only his brain, guide him to the
world championship. Of course, all this made Taylor sound like a loser to
begin with, but the worst was yet to come.

Heenan claimed that Taylor didn't even deserve a name, and instead,
Heenan stated, he would just be his "Little Red Rooster." And, sure enough,
he was billed as "The Red Rooster" from that point on in his WWF career.
Heenan, upon seeing the Rooster lose match after match, began to browbeat his employee. Finally, Taylor broke away, becoming his own man.

Heenan was furious, and he engaged his former employee in a debate
in which he said that Taylor shouldn't even call himself "Red Rooster" anymore, since that was a name Heenan had come up with. Taylor actually
disagreed. Not only did he continue to call himself Red Rooster, but he
actually began to act like a chicken as well! He spiked his hair and dyed it
red and began to peck and scratch upon entering the ring. His music consisted of cock-a-doodle-doo-ing and other farm sounds. Instead of rallying
to this barnyard buffoon's cause, fans simply laughed at him.

Taylor's career never recovered. Although the WWF and other promotions would eventually give him different gimmicks, fans would inevitably
chant "Rooster! Rooster!" when he would come to the ring. The Red Rooster
had completely destroyed his in-ring career.

Indeed, at times during the mid-'80s, it appeared as though McMahon
was simply throwing stuff against the wall to see what would stick. All
these crazy characters were just window dressing, however. They were bit
players in McMahon's production, and as one would fade in popularity, he
would simply create a new one to take his place. McMahon knew that there
was just one star of this show: Hulk Hogan. Arena attendance confirmed

Cock-a-doodle-doo! Say hello to pro wrestling's answer to Foghorn Leghorn, the Red Rooster.

that fact. When Hogan was advertised on the card, the arena would sell out. If he wasn't, attendance would suffer.

Throughout the mid-to-late 1980s, Hogan sold out arenas the world over. He headlined every major WWF pay-per-view. He appeared on the cover of *Sports Illustrated*. He made the WWF—and himself—millions and millions of dollars. His complete dominance of the industry during this period cannot be understated.

But as the 1980s drew to a close, the Hulkster's popularity began to wane. Before this became too noticeable, Hogan decided that he'd had enough of the wrestling business. He had already conquered the world. What else was there left to do, aside from fade into oblivion? He had been champion, and therefore the focal point of the promotion, for years. It was time, he reasoned, to branch out and see just how a big a star he could be.

And there was only one place to do that: Hollywood.

You Oughtn't Be in Pictures

Despite the success he had achieved in the WWF, Hulk Hogan wanted more. He wanted the money and fame that only being a movie star could bring. Actually, he already was a movie star. Hogan had a couple of bit parts under his belt prior to the explosion of Hulkamania in the mid-1980s, and given pro wrestling's tendency to exaggerate, that was equivalent to being the next Arnold Schwarzenegger.

For years, many people have believed that Hogan's acting debut was in a film called *Michael Nesmith's Elephant Parts*. You remember Michael Nesmith, right? He was the guy who wore the wool hat in The Monkees. Apparently, the producers of the show even wanted to name him "Michael Woolhat," proving that stupidity isn't limited to the wrestling business.

Nesmith had inherited about $50 million from his mother, who had become wealthy by inventing liquid paper. Nestmith took the cash and decided to enter the world of motion pictures. *Elephant Parts* was basically just a series of skits and music videos that was released as the world's first "video record." It achieved a degreee of cult notoriety, and even won the first-ever Grammy award for a video.

The kicker was that it wasn't Hogan actually in the role, but a Hogan lookalike named Steven Strong. Though this Hogan impersonator was only in the film briefly, it ironically gave the real Hogan some level of publicity, which helped him land a major role in the upcoming *Rocky III*.

With *Rocky III*, Hogan truly hit the big time. In the film, he didn't stretch much beyond what he knew. He portrayed a wrestler known as Thunderlips, and he came to the ring wearing boas and a big pimp hat. He was scheduled to face off with Rocky in a special boxer-vs.-wrestler charity brawl. Rocky asked Thunderlips to "make it look good," and Thunderlips happily obliged by throwing the Italian Stallion all over the ring.

Rocky III was a hit, with critics raving about Hogan's performance in particular. The opportunity also allowed Hogan to meet some powerful folks within Hollywood, such as Sylvester Stallone and Mr. T. This led to more work, including stints on Mr. T's television show, *The A-Team*. With the success of *Rocky III*, it was no shock that Hogan was snatched up a year or so later by the WWF. McMahon loved what he saw in Hogan and was also able to sign Mr. T for a handful of shows, including the initial *Wrestlemania* telecast.

Once Hogan had been firmly established in the media thanks to the success of *Wrestlemania*, the next logical step was to exploit his popularity beyond the traditional wrestling venues. Vince decided to ramp up the cartoonish aspects of his company and play to the children's market, going so far as to have a Saturday-morning cartoon created by DIC Entertainment. *Hulk Hogan's Rock 'n' Wrestling* debuted on CBS television on September 14, 1985, and ran through the '85 and '86 seasons. The cartoon highlighted all the WWF superstars of the day, giving them even greater exposure to their target audience. None of the wrestlers did their own voices, but if you listen closely to the episodes, you may recognize the man who did the voice of the Hulkster as Brad Garrett, who plays Robert Barone on the CBS comedy hit *Everybody Loves Raymond*.

As the '80s came to a close, Hogan made the decision to get back on the big screen, this time in a starring role. It was quite a leap for someone who had spent the last five years on the road, acting only in wrestling interviews, in which he called everyone "dude" or "brother." The film was entitled *No Holds Barred*, and it was released on June 2, 1989. In an effort to ensure its success, Hogan and McMahon produced the film themselves, and they also did a fair amount of work on the script. The film was promoted heavily on WWF television.

In it, Hogan portrays WWF champion Rip Thomas, the number-one ratings draw in television. (Yep, this was definitely written by Hogan and McMahon.) Networks all over the world want his services, including the evil World Television Network, headed by the vile and reprehensible Mr. Brell. Livid at being dead last in the ratings, Brell demands that Rip join his network. Much to Brell's chagrin, Rip has given his word to his current network and declines Brell's offer. Brell, furious at the snub, devises a diabolical scheme to get Rip on his network.

His first plan is to kidnap Rip in a limousine that has been reinforced with metal windows. Rip attempts to kick the door off, and he kicks with such force that his footprints are visible from outside the vehicle. Those are some strong feet! The car finally screeches to a halt inside an abandoned parking garage. The thugs close in on the vehicle, and suddenly Rip smashes the roof off the limo and springs ten feet into the air. A horrible pro-wrestling-style fight occurs, in which Rip headbutts and clotheslines his lead-pipe-wielding assailants into submission. Rip's fury causes the driver to poop his pants in sheer terror. This special moment is illustrated not only with a close-up of the man's soiled pants, but this fantastic dialogue as well:

Rip (growling): "What's that smelllllll?"

Villain (in tears): "Doo . . . dookie."

Coming to the realization that felonious assault is probably not the best method of operation, Brell hires Samantha Moore (Joan Severance) in an attempt to seduce our hero. However, few women can resist the charms of a greased-up Hulk Hogan, and Sam is no exception. She begins falling for the big guy after he stops an armed robbery by starting a pie fight. Don't ask. She eventually gives it up after watching Rip work out in a thong, a love scene the world hasn't seen the likes of since. Thank God.

After seeing his best people either moisten their panties or crap their drawers at the mighty aura of Rip, Brell unleashes his own wrestling-style show, *Battle of the Tough Guys*, a no-holds-barred competition in which rednecks fight to the death for the grand prize of $100,000. Zeus (Tiny Lister), a cross-eyed black behemoth who has just been released from prison, eventually wins the contest. Apart from beating people to bloody pulps, Zeus's primary hobby seems to be screaming, which he does constantly throughout the film.

Battle of the Tough Guys catapults Brell's network to number one, but that isn't enough: he wants total world domination, the likes of which can only be brought about by pitting Zeus against Rip. Our hero ignores the challenges, until Zeus shows up at a charity sack race and beats Rip's weakling brother Randy into paralysis.

Finally, our hero can take no more, and he agrees to meet Zeus to settle things once and for all. In order to ensure Zeus's victory, Brell kidnaps Samantha and instructs Zeus to go after Randy, who is sitting ringside in a wheelchair, at the earliest opportunity. After an arduous battle, Rip is able to gain the upper hand, throwing Zeus off a catwalk forty feet in the air. He falls into the ring, which collapses. Rip then turns his rage toward Brell, who falls backward into a live circuit box and gets electrocuted. The movie ends with Rip, Randy, and Sam celebrating their victory, and everyone lives happily ever after.

Except, of course, for Zeus and Brell, since they're dead.

The movie was a huge hit, or so the WWF would have had you believe. Commentator Bobby Heenan claimed that he hadn't even been able to get in to see it, as the lines were around the block. Play-by-play man Gorilla Monsoon claimed that people were talking Oscar for Hogan's performance.

Reality was a little less kind. The film drew just $16 million at the box office, or roughly what *Rocky III* had made during its opening weekend alone. The reviews weren't good, either, as critics universally panned Hogan's wooden performance. Chris Hicks, of the *Deseret News*, wrote, "Hogan has two expressions: Grimacing and not grimacing."

Despite the fact that the movie was both a critical and financial flop, the WWF decided to bring the lead villain into the ring. Zeus began showing up at live events, challenging Hogan to fights. This led to a pair of pay-per-view encounters in which Zeus teamed with Hogan nemesis Randy Savage in an effort to keep the matches from stinking the arenas up too badly.

For some reason, other producers looked at *No Holds Barred* and began offering Hogan movie roles. His next feature was *Suburban Commando*, in which he played intergalactic warrior Shep Ramsey. After he botches a rescue mission in the deep recesses of space, Shep finds his craft is damaged and in need of recharging. His supervisors order him to land on Earth and then kick back and relax for the six weeks it will take for the ship to repair itself.

Shelley Duvall and Christopher Lloyd costar as a married couple attempting to make ends meet by renting out a room to Shep. Lloyd plays a cowardly architect, and Long is his sexually frustrated wife. You know, you really haven't experienced torture until you've seen Olive Oyl (decked out in a Victoria's Secret nightie and a whore wig) attempt to seduce Doc Brown.

With the couple's help, Ramsey attempts to blend in with the locals by attacking the mailman with a knife and propelling the paperboy into the shrubs. Eventually, he uses his superhuman strength for the good of the community, saving children from traffic accidents, retrieving stolen purses, and beating up mimes. Seriously — an entire subplot is centered on Ramsey pummeling pasty-faced clowns. Before he can become too comfortable, however, a pair of bounty hunters tracks him down, leading to a final show-down in which Lloyd's character grows a set and saves the day.

The film's "special effects" are laughable, at best. Hogan's commando suit is particularly cheesy; a third-grader with decent art skills could come up with something better using a cardboard box, some paint, and a couple of tin cans. The spaceships look to have come from the clearance aisle at the local Toys "R" Us. And the less said about the scenes in which Hogan skateboards, the better.

Suburban Commando was a marginally better film than *No Holds Barred*, but that didn't keep it from bombing. It made less than $7 million at the box office. The reviews were harsh. Roger Ebert went so far as to claim that the film caused him to reconsider his chosen profession: "Somebody was asking the other day, do I ever get tired of going to the movies? Naw, I said, I love movies and so some days it's not really a job, it's more of a lucky break. But I wasn't feeling lucky the day I saw *Suburban Commando*, and you know what? By golly, by the time it was over, I was feeling kind of tired of going to the movies."

Hogan followed up *Suburban Commando* with the ridiculous *Mr. Nanny*. In this family adventure, Hogan portrays Sean Wilson, an out-of-work pro wrestler who is befriended by his old buddy Burt, played by Sherman Helmsley, who you might remember as George Jefferson. Sean, down on his luck and reluctant to return to the ring, is convinced by Burt to take up a job as a bodyguard. What Sean doesn't know is that the position is actually to oversee two feisty children who have made a living scaring off would-be nannies. The children's father, Mason, is a brilliant scientist who makes top-secret microchips. These chips guide special "laser rockets," which look just like regular rockets, but are designed to more closely resemble a penis. With this in mind, it is easy to understand why the family is need of security.

Mason is being hunted down by David Johansen, aka Buster Poindexter, crooner of "Hot Hot Hot." If you don't know that song, consider yourself lucky. It's the audio equivalent of having your toenails ripped off with pliers. Johansen, who plays Thanatos, the film's villain, sports a shiny metal plate on his head that causes him to have headaches and scream a lot. Good, healthy lungs that enable loud shrieking seem to be a requirement of all Hogan movie villains.

Mason's housekeeper dubs Sean "Mr. Nanny." Our hero does everything he can to protect the children, who in return do everything they can to harm him. They attempt to electrocute him and choke him with a barbell. Finally, he snaps, screaming at the children, which is something their father has never done. Miraculously, this causes the children to fall in love with Mr. Nanny, viewing him as the verbally abusive father they never had.

The kids begin to let their newfound friend play all manner of games with them, the highlight of which is Hogan dressing up in a pink tutu and drinking tea. The fun and frivolity is short-lived, however, as the Masons and Burt are kidnapped by Thanatos. In the end, Mr. Nanny saves the day with the help of the nerdy family. Mason creates a generator of sorts that spins Thanatos around and around, finally shooting him into outer space, perhaps in hopes of setting up Hogan's next film, *Mr. Nanny Versus Suburban Commando.*

To the shock of no one, *Mr. Nanny* drew even less money than *Suburban Commando* did, this time less than $5 million. Reviews, again, were brutal. James Berardinelli of ReelViews claimed it was "one of the most monstrously agonizing motion pictures to come along this year. *Mr. Nanny* isn't entertainment; it's an exercise in masochism."

But, as P.T. Barnum once said, "There's a sucker born every minute." Hogan proved this to be true by landing yet another movie, a holiday feature entitled *Santa with Muscles.*

The movie begins with Hogan sneaking up on a palatial estate. Suddenly, a horde of nogoodniks begins to attack him with various deadly weapons, including that most dreaded of weapons, the Weed Eater. Hogan fights back with dinner plates. We learn that the bad guys are actually in Hogan's employ, and that they attack him to keep him in shape. Hogan plays Blake, who, according to the film, is the "richest man in ten states." He's an egotistical jerk who shills nutritional goods, then complains about the size of his picture on the cans.

For fun, Blake likes to drive around in his jeep firing paintballs at pedestrians and cops, one of whom doesn't take kindly to this good-natured fun. In danger of being caught, Blake hides in a shopping mall and disguises himself in a Santa suit. He then falls down a shaft and gets amnesia. Yes, amnesia. When he wakes up, he really thinks he's Santa.

While Blake is inviting children to tell him what they want for Christmas, a couple of hoods try to steal donations intended for the local orphanage. Blake throws the children off his lap and springs into action. The bad guys (who are under the employ of an albino named Ebner Frost) attack him with giant Styrofoam candy canes, but Blake fights them off and returns the money to the children. As this is happening, Lenny the Evil Elf loots Blake's wallet, discovering his true identity. Lenny decides he can make some money off Santa and therefore befriends him.

Eventually, the pair winds up at what is likely the world's smallest orphanage. Inside are three children, a woman who oversees them, and Garrett Morris of *Saturday Night Live* fame. At this point, more of Frost's hoodlums show up in an ice cream truck and try to run over Garrett Morris, presumably for no reason other than the fact that he's Garrett Morris. Santa stops the truck by grabbing a chain and pulling with all his might, like in one of those "World's Strongest Man" competitions they show on ESPN2 at 3:30 in the morning. The newspapers get wind of this and dub our hero "Santa with Muscles"; hence the idiotic title of this idiotic film.

For no adequately explained reason, the children decide to go spelunking beneath the world's smallest orphanage. During this excursion, they find crystals made up of exploding gems. When Santa drops one, it explodes into a million pieces. Remember that, because it's important later.

Following yet another fight with Frost's goons, Santa with Muscles is thrown from a bell tower by an animatronic Santa. He lands in a garbage truck and winds up in his own bed. You see, the garbage men were the only people in the entire movie to recognize him, despite the fact that he's "the richest man in ten states"!

Blake, having regained his memory, reflects on a life misspent. He rushes back to the world's smallest orphanage in an attempt to set things right. By this time, however, Frost's evil misfits have taken over the building. Santa with Muscles is nothing if not resilient, however, and he defeats Frost's lackeys using the crane technique, just like in *The Karate Kid*. This leads to a final battle between Frost and Santa in the mine below the orphanage, with the pair having a sword fight using shards of crystals. The same crystals that blow up if you so much as touch them. During this sequence, they clank together for about ten minutes and nothing happens.

To ensure the requisite happy ending, Santa with Muscles defeats Frost. Suddenly, the crystals go nuclear and the mine starts to collapse. Everyone runs out to safety and the world's smallest orphanage implodes. As the film draws to a close, the orphanage residents move into Santa with Muscles's house. Not just the kids — *everyone*, including Garrett Morris (who is now Santa with Muscles's gardener) and Lenny the Evil Elf, who sunbathes.

Drawing less than $200,000 at the box office, *Santa with Muscles* surely should have signaled the end of Hulk Hogan's movie career. Instead, Hogan was given his own television show, *Thunder in Paradise*. Starring with Chris Lemmon and Carol Alt, Hogan took on the role of "Hurricane" Spencer, a former Navy Seal turned mercenary who hangs out on the beaches of south Florida. The plot sees Spencer in need of money to help pay for his super-high-tech boat, *Thunder*, which has a retractable shield, a missile launcher, and a stealth system that makes it undetectable to standard scanning systems. Think of the show as *Knight Rider* meets *Baywatch*, with Hulk Hogan instead of Pamela Anderson. Although their acting abilities and chest sizes are comparable, there's something not exactly fair about the trade-off.

The show was incredibly cheesy, featuring nickel-and-dime special effects. The idea was that wrestling fans would tune in just to see Hogan and his pals. In fact, other wrestlers appeared on the show on a nearly weekly basis, ranging from legitimate superstars such as Sting to WrestleCrappers like El Gigante. Never mind that these men had no real acting ability. After all, that never stopped the Hulkster!

Despite being promoted on Turner Network Television, the show lasted only one season before being canceled, leaving Hogan once again wondering just what to do with his career.

To be fair, it's not as if Hogan was the only wrestler to make bad movies. Heck, nearly every motion picture starring a wrestler or about wrestling was atrocious. Roddy Piper, for instance, actually preceded Hogan's first starring role by several years thanks to *Body Slam*, a film in which he portrayed (you guessed it) a wrestler.

Let's see what it says on the back of the movie case: "Harry Smilac is a talent agent who'd sell his mother for a dollar . . . fifty cents after negotiations. But Harry finally hits the big time with a rhythm and bruise road show that combines rock music and professional wrestling. Sound crazy? It is! In fact, *Body Slam* is the craziest, funniest, rock-ingest wrestling movie of all time!"

Now let's run that through our BS-to-English translator: "Dirk Benedict is an actor who'd sell his soul to the devil for a dollar . . . fifty cents after *The A-Team* went off the air and plans for a *Battlestar Galactica* reunion fell through. But Dirk finally hits rock bottom with a lame-ass movie that combines rock music and professional wrestling. Sound stupid? It is! In fact, *Body Slam* is the crappiest, most forgettable, suckiest wrestling movie of all time!"

In this celluloid piece of crap, Dirk Benedict stars as a rock & roll manager who, through the zaniest of circumstances, winds up managing Quick Rick (Roddy Piper) and Tonga Tom (Tonga Kid). This, of course, infuriates their former manager, Capt. Lou Morano (Lou Albano), so Lou's men attack Dirk's team, and Lou blackballs Rick and Tom from all the major arenas.

To overcome this situation, Benedict combines his two interests, wrestling and rock & roll, by merging Rick and Tom with some horribly bad '80s heavy metal band that makes Poison sound like Metallica. The whole clan together looks quite a bit like the Village People, actually. The crowds go crazy, of course. This leads to a big verbal showdown on *Ring Talk*, which is, according to Piper, the "highest rated show on television." And how could it not be? It's hosted by *Charles Nelson Reilly*, for crying out loud!

Predictably, Piper and Tonga get the match, they beat the bad guys, and Dirk Benedict fades back into obscurity. Everyone's a winner — except for the poor suckers watching this movie, which features bad music, worse wrestling, and even worse acting. The highlight of the movie for wrestling fans is a section near the end featuring two seconds of cameos by Ric Flair, Freddy Blassie, and Bruno Sammartino. Legendary midget actor Billy Barty calls Benedict a "faggot" for another three. And the guy that played Gomez Addams on *The Addams Family* TV show is in it for another five.

Hard though it may be to believe, those ten seconds aren't worth sitting through the movie's other 89 minutes and 46 seconds of pure crap.

Body Slam was directed by Hal Needham, a former stuntman who directed such other testosterone-filled classics as *Smokey and the Bandit* and *Cannonball Run*. While neither of those films was critically acclaimed, they both made tons of money, something his wrestling picture did not. *Body Slam* was a dud, and to this day, it is nearly impossible to find in even the largest video stores. Needless to say, Needham hasn't done much directing since *Body Slam* hit the theaters.

It was, however, the break Piper was looking for, and he went on to have a successful movie career. Well, at least as successful as Hulk Hogan's, which, admittedly, isn't saying a lot. Piper's next starring role was rather well received by both audiences and critics. *They Live*, directed by *Halloween*'s John Carpenter, stars Piper as John Nada, a homeless construction worker who has become disillusioned with American society. He finds a pair of sunglasses that literally open his eyes to what is going on in the world, and with their assistance he discovers that the world is besieged by political propaganda that is all but hidden from the naked eye.

It seems odd that a wrestler, especially one who had come from a film such as *Body Slam*, would be picked to star in a science fiction thriller with a rather deep social commentary. But that's just the case, and Piper was able to pull it off quite well. Though the movie only made $13 million during its initial run, that covered its budget three times over. Piper's performance was considered more than acceptable, and he was offered other movie and television roles.

Piper's next flick was the oddly titled *Hell Comes to Frogtown*, a post-apocalyptic story in which the human race is on the verge of extinction. Piper stars as Sam Hell, one of the few remaining fertile men and a prisoner of the army. He is offered freedom in exchange for impregnating the few remaining fertile human females on the planet. The catch? He has a bomb attached to his 'nads, and if he strays, it's *sayonara* to Jack and the Curly Q's. He is carted off to Frogtown, where he is to rescue (and then impregnate) a clan of ovulating women under the control of a mutant frog. The film featured Z-grade special effects and classic lines like, "Hey, you try making love in a hostile, mutant environment. See how you like it."

In other words, it was a big step down from *They Live*. His next role may have been one of the most interesting ever, if only because his costar was Jesse Ventura. The two were paired up for a television series called *Tag Team*, in which they starred as — gasp! — wrestlers who had been blackballed for refusing to lose a match, just like *Mr. Nanny*. The two go through a series of odd jobs, becoming piano movers and tackling dummies for a women's self-defense class, before finally settling on careers as police officers.

Sadly, while the pilot actually showed some promise, the series was never picked up, as ABC reportedly canceled it the day before it was to begin shooting its first regular-season episode. Piper headed back to the ring, while Ventura wound up on various radio programs before shocking the nation by becoming governor of Minnesota.

Not all movies about wrestling feature legitimate wrestlers. In fact, there is one infamous film about wrestling that doesn't even feature legitimate actors. In 1988, a company called Pleasure Productions out of New Jersey marketed *The Young and the Wrestling,* the world's first pro wrestling porno flick.

The "film" opens with Kimberly and Janice discussing Janice's extramarital affair. Stellar dialogue follows, as Kimberly whines, "I wish I was having an affair! My sex life is sooooo boring!" After swearing secrecy, they go into the living room, where their husbands, Melvin and Brad, are watching wrestling. This in itself wouldn't be so odd, save for the fact that the two are wearing thongs and nothing else.

The guys see a commercial for Wildman's Wild World of Wrestling School, and they decide that a career in pro wrestling is probably just what they need to pull them out of their doldrums. One would think that just getting up off the couch and putting on a pair of pants would improve things, but apparently the pirate wearing the eye patch in Wildman's commercial knows best. And really, who could argue with a guy getting a blow job from a hot blond in the middle of the ring? Especially as he hollers classic lines like, "Great balls of fire, have mercy, baby," and, "I love your lip lock, owwww!"

Melvin and Brad head off to the training academy, where they are given new personas. Melvin becomes Zulu the Voodoo Man, while nerdy

Brad transforms into Hunk Golden. The boys are taken into the back room by Princess Penelope, who proceeds to slurp their sausages. That's certainly an interesting training technique. One can only hope that this wasn't a regular part of the routine in Stu Hart's Dungeon.

The wives eventually find out about their husbands' escapades and decide that they, too, want jobs in the exciting world of pro wrestling. This sets up a tag team encounter with the guys against the girls. Pandemonium breaks loose, leading to a big orgy at the end of the film, as Wildman and Penelope look on like proud parents.

Then, very unlike proud parents, they too join the orgy.

Maybe *Mr. Nanny* wasn't so bad after all.

Warrior Wisdom

With Hulk Hogan off in Hollywood pretending to be a movie star, Vince needed an heir to the throne. He had attempted to find one in the ultra-popular Randy "Macho Man" Savage, and although business with Savage on top was good, Vince felt that a muscle man from Queens, New York, could boost interest and revenues even more. In hopes of creating the next Hulk Hogan, Vince signed Jim Hellwig to a long-term contract.

Hellwig had learned the wrestling business under the watchful eyes of Rick Bassman in California, who had a vision of creating a muscle-bound quartet known as Powerteam USA. The idea fell apart quickly, however, as two of the members left the business in short order. Hindsight being twenty-twenty, they might have been well advised to stay. Not only did Hellwig go on to become one of the most popular wrestlers in the world, but the other guy who stuck it out did as well. During his early days, Hellwig teamed with Steve Borden, who went on to become one of WCW's main draws: Sting.

After his brief stay on the West Coast, Hellwig and Borden split. Sting went to Bill Watts's UWF region, and Hellwig headed to the Lone Star State and the World Class territory, the province of the legendary Von Erich clan. Fritz, the eldest of the Von Erich crew and the lead booker, dubbed him the Dingo Warrior and claimed that he had been raised by Aborigines in

Australia. Maybe he was hanging out with Outback Jack. Come to think of it, that would have been a hell of a team. "On their way to the ring, at a total combined moves of three, Outback Jack and the Dingo Warrior!"

Hellwig wasn't long for Texas. Vince McMahon took one look at the guy's amazing physique, threw some bangles on his biceps and war paint on his face, and renamed him the Ultimate Warrior. The Warrior was instructed to run to the ring as quickly as possible, all the while acting like a complete madman — which, it later turned out, wasn't much of a stretch. Hellwig played his new shtick to the hilt, grabbing the ring ropes and shaking them as though electrical current coursed through his body. If it weren't for the fact that he was sculpted like an Adonis, he would have looked like a total buffoon.

The WWF made sure to protect its investment by having his matches last mere seconds, and Warrior annihilated every opponent in his path. That's one of the oldest tricks in wrestling, and it generally works. The theory is that if fans see a machine that tears opponents limb from limb, an instrument of destruction that never loses, they will get behind him. And if this newcomer can annihilate lower-card workers, surely he can crush top-of-the-card villains who the fans hate as well. Some of the biggest names in wrestling history have been created this way. The Road Warriors, Goldberg, and, to some extent, even Hulk Hogan, were pushed in exactly the same way, which paid dividends to the promotion doing the booking. "Always win, never lose" generally works.

Such was the case with the Warrior. He blew through the longest-reigning Intercontinental title holder on record, the Honky Tonk Man, in less than a minute. Fans gasped as he crushed all opponents using the simplest repertoire of moves imaginable, consisting primarily of a clothesline, body slam, and splash. It was something that every wrestling fan did to his little brother, only now a muscle-bound madman who growled and snarled through his interviews was performing it.

And his interviews were . . . interesting, to say the least. Whereas other wrestlers would run down their opponents, talking about all the nasty things they were going to do to them, Warrior would almost go into a trance, looking at his hands as though they had some kind of grasp on him. He would use ten-dollar words that went over most of his audience's head. One big snort later, the interview was over. During matches, he would look to the sky, to his "gods," as though he was seeking the answer to some mystical conundrum. Fans were definitely intrigued by the act.

Vince McMahon had enough faith in the Warrior to put him over his top draw of the last decade: the mighty Hulk Hogan himself. The two were set to square off at *Wrestlemania VI*, which would be in the cavernous SkyDome in Toronto. If anyone had a chance of filling the arena's 65,000-plus seats, it would surely be Warrior and Hogan.

And they did it. The event was a huge success, capped off with a main event that was far better than it had any right to be. The booking leading to the match, and the layout of the match itself, were done in such a way that neither man would be considered the villain. It worked. The end of the encounter saw Hogan congratulate Warrior for his victory in what was meant to be a legendary "passing of the torch" moment.

And, for a brief period, it was successful. Warrior's title win was a breath of fresh air in what had become a very stagnant WWF. The celebration was short-lived, however, as the WWF booking crew had forgotten to build up any strong heel for the Warrior to defend his title against after the big win.

So it was that a chiseled playboy by the name of "Ravishing" Rick Rude was given the nod. Rude had history on his side in the story line — he was the only guy to ever beat the Warrior. He had accomplished the feat at *Wrestlemania V*, with a liberal helping of outside interference from his manager, Bobby "The Brain" Heenan. This was really the only selling point of the feud, however, as Warrior had destroyed him in subsequent rematches. Rude slipped further down the card, involving himself in a feud with Roddy Piper, who had returned from retirement for the third or fourth time. Piper obliterated Rude as well.

After seeing Rude get routinely demolished over the previous year, fans had little reason to believe that he would pose any kind of threat to someone who had just cleanly pinned a man most fans considered the biggest icon in pro wrestling history. Past win or no, fans knew that Warrior would cream Rude, and they had little interest in these title defenses. The initial house-show run with Warrior on top was extremely disappointing, to the point that Hogan was brought back to coheadline the WWF's *SummerSlam* pay-per-view. But even with Hogan's help, the buy rate for the show was down significantly from the year before, which had been headlined by Hogan in a tag team match with lifetime midcarder Brutus Beefcake.

As attendance at house shows dwindled, the Warrior was thrown into six-man tag matches with hot WWF newcomers the Road Warriors in hopes of increasing crowds. That didn't really work either, so the WWF decided to take the belt off the Warrior as quickly as possible. The dethroning would take place at the *Royal Rumble* in January of 1991.

For those of you who know your world history, you probably recall this as a time when the United States was about to enter the first Gulf War. Never one to miss out on the chance to highjack a passing bandwagon, McMahon decided to bring back Bob Remus, known to longtime fans as Sgt. Slaughter. Slaughter was a military character who always fought for the good ol' U.S. of A. He was a GI Joe come to life. In fact, he actually starred —as himself—in the GI Joe cartoon that aired in the late 1980s.

This time around, though, McMahon wasn't bringing back the Sarge to combat evil foreigners. Instead, Slaughter was turned heel, claiming that his country had deserted him and that he was proclaiming his loyalty to Saddam Hussein and Iraq. The thought that American forces were about to invade the region and that many young men would likely die appeared to mean little to Vinnie Mac, especially when he could turn that xenophobia into cold, hard cash. One knock to the noggin later, and Warrior was just another former world champ, another failed experiment in a book filled with them.

While few would argue that, from a business perspective, the Warrior's title reign was anything but a total flop, the WWF still felt that he could be a draw. Maybe, just maybe, they needed to ratchet up his increasingly bizarre persona in battles against other far-out combatants. Therefore, Warrior was put into a feud with the man from the dark side himself, the Undertaker. The original Undertaker gimmick was that he was an undead zombie of some sort himself, who could not be harmed by mortal men. Led to the ring by his manager, Paul Bearer (get it?), Undertaker was himself an unstoppable force. He derived supernatural powers from an urn that contained the remains of someone he either murdered or called "Mommy and Daddy," depending on the whim of the WWF when they told the story.

Those of you who are reading this book and have no prior knowledge of pro wrestling history are probably laughing yourselves silly thinking that of all the idiotic gimmicks so far described in this book, none could possibly have bombed worse than this. An undead zombie who drew magic power from an urn? Puh-leaze.

Those of you who do know your wrestling, though, are well aware of the fact that the whole façade not only succeeded, it succeeded for over 10 years, making it one of the longest-lasting gimmicks in pro wrestling history. Wrestling's strange like that—sometimes the things that make the most sense bomb, while ideas that look idiotic on paper go on to draw big money. That's likely why there have been so many silly angles and characters over the years: you never know when something will click with the fans.

The setup for the Warrior-Undertaker feud was way, way out there. Bearer and Undertaker were the hosts of a weekly segment called "The Funeral Parlor," in which they interviewed wrestlers about their intentions in a spookhouse setting. Think of it as "Piper's Pit," but replace Roddy Piper with a fat, short, pale-faced man who spoke in a high-pitched, ghostly voice of his desire to embalm his enemies. Family fun for everyone! One week, they invited the Warrior to their weekly ghoul gab and promised him a gift.

But it wasn't just any gift—it was his own brand new, custom-made casket! (Can't you just imagine hearing *The Price Is Right*'s Rod Roddy screaming that?) This baby was decked out with all the finest accessories any cadaver might need, along with the latest in undead fashion chic: tiny Warrior symbols! It's surprising that upon seeing this the Warrior didn't hop right in and declare himself legally dead.

Instead, he needed Undertaker to convince him to do so with an urn shot to the back of the head. Bearer and Undertaker then sealed the casket and threw away the key, laughing as they left the set. WWF emergency personnel flooded the scene, attempting to pry open the casket any way they could. Among the more inventive tools used were a drill and a hammer. Maybe they thought they could pound it open? Finally, after nearly ten minutes locked inside the airtight casket, Warrior was rescued.

When they opened the casket they discovered that Warrior had passed out and was grasping the lining of the casket's lid. For all the goofy setup to the feud, this attack proved one thing: that Warrior was, in fact, human and could be hurt. And the first guy really prove this was the Undertaker. With this, the WWF had successfully woven together several tried-and-true formulas for making money, combining the babyface destruction machine who could not be stopped with a nefarious rule breaker who proved the face actually could be stopped, and that the rule breaker was just the guy to do it.

Warrior and Undertaker embarked on a series of "body bag" matches. The goal of these contests was to shove your opponent into a body bag like the ones the morgue uses to zip up stiffs. While those outside the industry would be appalled by such an event (especially given that at this time the WWF was still marketing primarily to children), for pro wrestling it was just a new way to convince fans to buy tickets—another day at the office, so to speak. Warrior and Taker split the series of matches pretty evenly, which led to a story arc in which Warrior began doubting himself and his gods. He needed something—or someone—to help him beat Undertaker at his own evil game.

Enter Jake "The Snake" Roberts, a man with a pretty decent dark side himself. Roberts entered the WWF as a rule breaker, splattering the head of longtime babyface Ricky Steamboat on the concrete floor. He was an immediate hit with fans, and it didn't take long for McMahon to figure out that those scattered cheers for the villainous Roberts could be made more abundant by simply having the guy attack heels instead. Of course, that would also lead to more T-shirt and poster sales, which is undoubtedly why the WWF decided to steer Roberts's career in this direction.

Roberts had turned face around *Wrestlemania III*. While his early feuds as a good guy, such as one with Rick Rude in which the Ravishing One painted a picture of Roberts's wife's face on the crotch of his tights, had been hot, his more recent ones had fizzled. Most notably, Roberts had been feuding with Rick Martel, a veteran French Canadian grappler who had been dubbed "The Model" by the WWF booking crew. He wore fancy clothes, claiming to be, well, a model. Just in case anyone doubted that he was, in fact, a model, he wore a big button on his outfits that read: "Yes, I Am a Model." So there can be little doubt that Rick Martel was a model.

In addition to a button proclaiming his occupation, he also carried around an old-style atomizer that contained Arrogance, his custom-made cologne. Whenever he was around someone who offended his refined olfactory senses, he would spray them with this water du toilet, much as Gorgeous George had done years earlier. One day, Martel happened to be in the company of Roberts whom The Model felt was rather stinky. Martel attempted to spray Roberts but accidentally on purpose sprayed him in the eyes. Roberts was blinded and spent months trying to regain his eyesight. At one point, he even wore a completely white contact lens over his left eye, which made it appear to fans at home that, by God, he really was blind. All this epic buildup led to a "blindfold" match, in which the combatants wore hoods over their heads so they couldn't see. That took even the silliness of pro wrestling to new depths, and it did little for Roberts or Martel's careers in the long run.

With the failure of the Martel feud, Roberts was understandably eager to lead Warrior down the path to the dark side. He set up a whole satanic regimen for his new pupil to follow. For starters, Jake decided that Warrior had to overcome his fear of the coffin. Jake nabbed the casket that Taker and Bearer had used to nearly kill Warrior, and convinced Warrior that it was in his best interest to get back in there. Jake then sealed the casket as the Warrior screamed like a little girl. A little girl who was being suffocated, that is.

Next, Roberts took Warrior out to the cemetery. Over the years, countless promoters have attempted to do wrestling skits in graveyards. A bit of free advice for future bookers: this never, *ever* works. Whether it be Warrior and Jake, Vampiro and KISS demon in WCW, whatever. Don't do it. It's idiotic, and nothing good has ever come of it. Be that as it may, Warrior and Jake did venture out to the graveyard. The Snake convinced Warrior that, in order to head to Evilville, he really needed to be buried alive. So Warrior jumped into a hole and allowed Roberts to shovel dirt all over his writhing carcass, all the while screaming, "Bury me, Snake Man! Bury me!" The scene ended with a skull facing Warrior's head, which was sticking slightly out of the mud as though it were some bizarre plant awaiting harvest.

This led to the climax, where Jake led the Ultimate One into a gigantic tomb and convinced him he needed to enter a hidden room to find the key to beating the Undertaker. Warrior traipsed into the room, only to find about a thousand snakes slithering all over the floor. Too dumb to figure out that this just might be a trap, Warrior headed for the center of the room, where he discovered a tiny casket. He very carefully opened it to discover a plastic snake smiling — literally smiling — back at him.

The synthetic snake leapt at the Warrior, in as much as a snake thrown by someone just out of range of the camera can be said to leap. Warrior writhed about in severe discomfort, finally collapsing to the ground in front of Roberts and his newfound friends, Undertaker and Paul Bearer. It was, of course, all a trap; "The Snake" had been on the wrong side of the tracks all along. Who'da thunk it?

This should have set up for a big feud between Roberts and the Warrior, and that was indeed what the promotion was counting on. Behind the scenes, though, Warrior was feeling increasingly dejected at being pushed farther and farther away from the world title and the money the main event slots promised. After teaming with Hulk Hogan at *SummerSlam '91*, Warrior vanished. Fans didn't know where he'd disappeared to, and they weren't going to get their answers from the WWF, as the company was none too happy about Warrior going AWOL.

After seven months in exile, Warrior returned to save Hulk Hogan from a two-on-one ambush at *Wrestlemania VIII*. At some point, a rumor was started that lingers to this day. The story goes that the Warrior died in real life, and that is why he was no longer around. When Warrior returned, he had changed his hairstyle somewhat, and this was proof enough to many in the crowd that the original Warrior was in fact dead, and that this new one was a phony. Some fans even went so far as to come to the conclusion that Kerry Von Erich, who had spent time with Warrior during his Texas years, was under the face paint. So, for what the writer of this book hopes will be (but, unfortunately, surely won't be) the final time, let's get this straight: this is *not* the case. The Ultimate Warrior always has been, and always will be, the same guy: Jim Hellwig. Maybe now that it is out there in printed form, someone will believe this.

Regardless of the rumor, Warrior was back on the scene, and he had returned with quite a bit more power than he had when he left. This was due in large part to Hulk Hogan, who had once again decided to step away from wrestling. The WWF even teased that Hogan's match at *Wrestlemania VIII* would be his final match ever, in the hopes of getting a few more fence-sitters to order the pay-per-view. With Hogan gone, the WWF had somewhat of a dearth of top babyfaces. WWF World Champion Randy Savage was sitting atop the throne, and few other headliners were available. Warrior was therefore given more or less carte blanche with his character, and he decided that the only way fans would truly believe his opponents were worthy of feuding with him would be if they had magic powers.

And thus Papa Shango, wrestling voodoo master, was born. With his face covered in white makeup to look like a skull, and wearing a top hat and furry coat, Shango was quite the sight. In fact, he could have passed as a muscle-bound stunt double for Baron Samedi, the James Bond villain from the 1973 film *Live and Let Die*.

But Shango didn't just look the part. He could actually back up his boasts with vile magic spells. He would speak in tongues, "cursing" his opponents. No, he didn't call Jim Powers a "dipshit" in Swahili. Rather, he would look into the smoking skull he carried to ringside and begin to chant. That's when bad things would happen. One opponent's hand caught on fire. An announcer had black goo ooze from his head. And as the crème de la crappe, he made the Ultimate Warrior puke right in front of a nationwide audience. So the feud was set: Warrior vs. Shango. Muscle-bound madman who stares at his hands against snake-charming witch doctor. Surely this was a feud for the ages!

The WWF, however, wasn't completely sold on the idea and had Warrior demolish Shango in short order.

Shango was demoted, but the company liked what they saw in the guy who played him, Charles Wright. What they saw was a huge black muscle man who had little skill in the ring but would do virtually whatever he was told without complaining. Therefore, every attempt was made to get him over with the wrestling audience. He was made into a UFC-style shoot fighter named Kama Mustafa, the Supreme Fighting Machine. A good rule of thumb about wrestling names is that if your moniker sounds like a punctuation mark, you probably won't succeed. And to the shock of literally no one, he didn't. So he was turned into The Godfather, a pimp who talked about lighting up fatties and doing the nasty with hos. This did get him over to some extent, and Wright to this day uses the gimmick on shows now and again. To show their appreciation for his years of service without complaint, the WWF gave Wright a brief Intercontinental title run in 1999.

Unlike Wright, who kept his job for years because he was willing to play along with every goofy angle that the WWF foisted upon him, Warrior made trouble behind the scenes. After the Papa Shango misfire, the WWF pushed the Warrior back up to the top of the card, and into a one-shot feud with Randy Savage. Both were babyfaces, and the promotion thought that if they were to turn the Warrior heel, they could generate some big money. Warrior vetoed the idea, thinking that the turn would cost him not only fans, but merchandising money as well. Due to his unwillingness to turn, the WWF decided they would move him back down the card again, this time against the evil convict Nailz in a series of matches in which the goal was to strap your opponent into an electric chair.

Upon hearing this news, Warrior quit the WWF. Of course, he did so just days before the annual *Survivor Series* pay-per-view, which historically had been one of the biggest shows of the year. The WWF had to shuffle the card, pulling a retired Mr. Perfect, Curt Hennig, back into the ring in Warrior's place. Warrior had vanished again.

Nailz was an interesting case as well. He seemed like a standard character, and he was ideal for a typical wrestling feud. He was a convict who had been locked away in the Cobb County Jail and was about to be released from his cell. He was headed for the WWF, and his target was his former

JEFF COHEN

Supposed convict Nailz practices his chokehold on a hapless opponent. He would later perfect the move in a backstage confrontation with Vince McMahon.

prison guard, Big Boss Man, whom Nailz claimed had beat him while he was in the slammer.

Little did anyone know that what was to go on behind the scenes would be much more interesting—and even more like a wrestling story line—than what actually took place in the ring. It seems that Kevin Wacholz, who played Nailz, was interested in becoming a jailbird himself.

Shortly after the *Survivor Series* that Warrior had no-showed, Wacholz approached Vince McMahon behind the scenes, upset about his payoff for *SummerSlam '92*. The argument became heated. Wacholz physically attacked McMahon, according to some accounts throttling him and scaring the living bejeebers out the owner of the WWF. He was blackballed from wrestling for years to come.

Or would have been, had it not been for the fact that WCW head Eric Bischoff loved the thought of Vince getting strangled. Bischoff brought Wacholz into WCW under a one-year deal as "The Convict," a gimmick that lasted a handful of matches and was then shelved forever, probably due to a WWF lawsuit claiming that the Convict character was too close to the Nailz character.

Wacholz's only other real claim to fame had to do with the infamous steroid trials of the early '90s—he was one of the few witnesses who was quite vocal in his testimony against the WWF. He was a little too vocal, in fact; ironically, his volatile testimony helped McMahon get off the hook. Wacholz's testimony was basically ignored as sour grapes from a bitter former employee. And who could blame them when one of his key statements was, "I hate Vince McMahon's guts"?

As for the Warrior, he and the WWF engaged in various legal battles, and he didn't return to the company until 1996, when the company was on the verge of being surpassed in the Monday-night wars against an upstart show called *WCW Nitro* on Ted Turner's TNT network. McMahon hit the panic button, bringing the Warrior back at his huge asking price. Warrior made his first appearance in a WWF ring in almost four years at *Wrestlemania XII*, still looking as muscular and out-of-control as ever. He destroyed a young Hunter Hearst Helmsley, then went on to feud with Jerry Lawler in matches best forgotten. While Warrior's appearance did spike ratings initially, it did very little in the long run. Warrior and the WWF began to bicker behind the scenes once again, this time over the promotion of Warrior's wrestling school and his comic books, one of which included Warrior putting Santa Claus into bondage. The less said about those items, the better. Warrior then left the promotion again for the final, *final* time.

At least as of this writing.

In an interesting twist, 1998 saw Bischoff's *Nitro* losing steam against McMahon's revitalized *Raw*. And this time it was Bischoff who turned to the Warrior in hopes of popping the ratings. Hulk Hogan was also behind the move; after all, this would allow Hogan to finally defeat one of the few guys who had ever got the upper hand on him.

Much as he'd done for McMahon two years earlier, the Warrior spiked the ratings and fan interest during his initial appearances with WCW. Then the goofiness began. Warrior—or WCW, or someone in charge—decided that the Warrior should become the second coming of Batman, complete with illuminated "Warrior Signal" and appeals to fans to tune in the following week at the "Same Warrior Time, Same Warrior Channel!"

This new Warrior could disappear at will. Audiences thrilled as Warrior would enter a ring, be doused with fire extinguishers, then magically vanish. Audiences may have loved it (well, actually, they didn't), but the wrestlers hated the trapdoors that were embedded in the rings for Warrior's tricks. In fact, Davey Boy Smith landed incorrectly on one of the doors and spent months in the hospital. Eric Bischoff then fired Smith via FedEx while he was still in traction. Who says wrestling promoters have no heart?

According to the story line, Hogan was unraveling thanks to the Warrior's mind games. Warrior set Hogan's dressing room on fire then kidnapped longtime Hogan lackey Ed Leslie (aka Brutus Beefcake) and turned him into a manservant. It was all very strange and vaguely homoerotic.

Things really went wacky on the October 5, 1998 edition of *Nitro*. Hogan was in his dressing room, looking in the mirror, when who should suddenly appear but the Warrior? Here's the catch: Warrior appeared to Hogan *in the mirror*, and no one else could see him. It was the Ultimate Mind Game!

Except, of course, for the fact that everybody could see Warrior in the mirror — Hogan, the fans at home, the announcers, everyone. Inexplicably, even Ray Charles saw the guy. Everyone saw Warrior in the mirror except for Eric Bischoff, who kept asking Hogan who he was talking to, what he saw. Idiot.

This led up to Warrior-Hogan II at *Halloween Havoc '98*. While every second of their *Wrestlemania VI* match had been plotted out in minute detail, this one wasn't . . . and boy could you tell. The match was well south of abysmal, and despite having two of the biggest wrestling stars of the past 15 years in front of them, the fans in Las Vegas nearly booed them out of the building. The finish was to see Hogan throw a fireball into Warrior's face, but it took the Hulkster nearly two minutes to manage a tiny spark that wouldn't have lit a cigarette. Warrior was finally subdued, however, and Hogan had defeated his hated rival.

And that's about it. Ratings had dropped back down to pre-Warrior levels. In a shocking turn of events, Warrior got upset with his treatment in WCW and vanished shortly after the Hogan match, presumably into a big cloud of smoke. Outside of a couple of indy appearances, he has not returned to the wrestling ring.

He did, at some point, change his name legally to "Ultimate Warrior." Almost makes you feel sorry for telemarketers who call his house. "Hello, is Mr. Warrior there? Can I call you Ultimate?" He remains in the public eye, as it were, via his Web site, ultimatewarrior.com. If you're ever having a rough time getting to sleep, or you're really, *really* stoned, you should check it out. His commentaries are certainly . . . interesting. The passages seldom relate to wrestling, but rather his views on life, politics, you name it. He's commented on everything from education to Evel Knievel.

He preaches a belief in one's inner being, which he calls "Warrior Wisdom." He has fabricated his own vocabulary to assist in his teachings. Think of it as sniglets for the clinically insane. For example, he has coined the term "destrucity." Here is Warrior's definition, as taken from his comic book: "Destrucity: In its design, Destrucity represents a constellation existing in the heavens which symbolizes the "Eight Disciplines" by which Warriors choose to live their lives. Brought to existence by the destinies of those willing to die for their Beliefs, brought to exist as a place where people live by Belief in the evolution of their Higher Selves — constantly evolving toward a completion of their chosen destiny — all with strength in the denial of "System Beliefs" — the very Beliefs that amplify differences in and create rights, wrongs, judgments, and opinions of people, places, and things."

And, really, what more can be said?

Other than this one public outlet, however, Warrior has remained an elusive figure, hoping to perpetuate his legend. No doubt he rests easily each night, knowing that eventually another promoter desperate for a short-term ratings fix will call, check in hand.

From deepest, darkest Africa comes Kamala. Originally an evil cannibal, he would later be 'civilized' by Reverend Slick and become quite the bowler.

Time traveler turned Oriental hitman, Yoshi Kwan.

Elvis wishes he could look this good: the ever gracious Honky Tonk Man.

Big Josh: lumberjack and bear dance partner.

Evil tax accountant, Irwin R. Schyster. IRS, get it? And yes, he did wrestle with his tie on. What a professional.

WCW did their best to cover the musical gamut by introducing headbangin' "Heavy Metal" Van Hammer (the only hard rocker who couldn't play the guitar)...

...and Little Richard wannabe Johnny B. Badd, who was most certainly Tutti Frutti.

In an effort to cross promote movies and wrestling, Kevin Nash was turned into the Great and Powerful Oz. Despite the best efforts of all involved (including a trained monkey), this plan flopped.

Max Moon: spaceman from Uranus, ribbed for her pleasure.

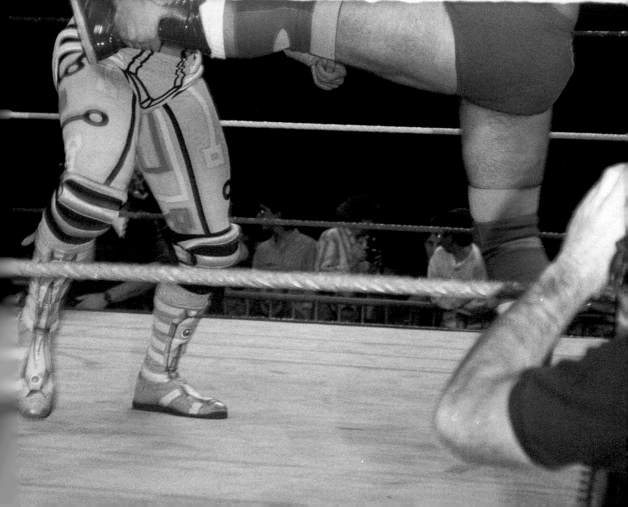

The Undertaker has arrived! No, wait, that's the Underfaker. You can tell them apart since the phony is six inches shorter than the real deal.

Garbage man by day, pro wrestler by night:
Duke "The Dumpster" Droese.

It appears as if Repo Man is about to get his nads repossessed.

Arriba! El Matador could defeat any bull, save for his own gimmick.

'El Gigante was bad enough in the WCW as Argentina's tin foil lovin' wrestling representative...

...but was many times worse after the WWF dressed him up as Sasquatch and dubbed him Giant Gonzalez.

Welcome to Oz! Welcome to Oz!

As dominant as the Ultimate Warrior was during his heyday, the WWF was even more powerful in the 1980s. Vince McMahon's company was able to more or less eliminate promotions at will during this period. However, there were a couple of groups that momentarily held off the charge: the American Wrestling Alliance (AWA) and the National Wrestling Alliance (NWA).

The AWA ran shows mainly in the Midwest, with its home operation based out of Minneapolis. Since the 1960s, the group had been home to many of the top stars in the country. Legends such as Larry Zbyszko, Nick Bockwinkle, Crusher, Dick the Bruiser, Hulk Hogan, Bobby Heenan, and many others all competed for Verne Gagne's promotion. The company had gained so much clout, in fact, that they were able to land a deal with ESPN for a daily TV show.

As the 1980s came to a close, though, things began to look more than a bit bleak for the company. Indeed, by 1990, McMahon had raided most of Gagne's best talent. Men who had been the cornerstone of the company, like Curt Hennig, Marty Jannetty, and Shawn Michaels, departed for the bigger paydays of the World Wrestling Federation. With attendance reaching nearly laughable levels, Gagne turned the booking over to a junior announcer by the name of Eric Bischoff, who announced the last great hope for the company: the Team Challenge Series.

Bischoff was confident that the concept would revolutionize the industry. The Team Challenge Series placed all the remaining wrestlers in the promotion into three separate teams, headed up by Larry Zbyszko, Sgt. Slaughter, and Baron von Raschke, the company's three main draws. After an unspecified amount of time, the winners would receive a million bucks.

Due to the fact that no fans were coming out to the events, the AWA made up a story about how there was too much interference in their matches, and thus they moved all the matches to an empty arena. Well, it wasn't really an arena, per se, but rather a big pink room. And the matches in the series weren't just any bouts, no sirree. They included such mythical concoctions as the "Behind the 8-Ball Battle Royal" and "The Great American Turkey Hunt."

Shockingly, the sight of two grown men fighting over a raw turkey in a giant salmon-colored warehouse didn't bring fans back to the arenas. After more than 30 years in the pro wrestling business, the AWA folded with a barely a whimper.

McMahon's remaining competitor was a bit more competent. Not much, but a little. They were the NWA, based primarily in the Carolinas. The NWA, with longtime promoter Jim Crockett at the helm, was easily Vince's largest competitor.

As was the case with the AWA, however, Crockett's talent base began to migrate north as Vince signed away as much NWA talent as he could. The wrestlers who remained were under hefty deals, and with attendance dwindling, Crockett was almost ready to pull the plug. Just when it looked like Vince would finally achieve the wrestling monopoly he had long dreamed of, Ted Turner, who aired NWA wrestling on his WTBS Superstation, stepped in and bought Crockett out. It just made sense—wrestling always provided high ratings for his networks, and it was, at the time, fairly inexpensive programming. Plus, Ted was a mark at heart.

After being purchased by Turner in 1990, Crockett's promotion, now referred to as World Championship Wrestling (WCW), struggled to find its identity. Fans had long viewed the WWF as a circus and the NWA as "real wrestling" — or at least as real as hitting someone over the head with a chair to win a match can be. While there was the occasional oddball gimmick, such as "Lasertron" (based on the popular laser-tag game of the day) or the New Breed (time travelers from the year 2002, one of whom later became an Oriental hitman by the name of Yoshi Kwan), the promotion was, by and large, built around a more realistic approach to wrestling. And there was no one better at this style of wrestling than "Nature Boy" Ric Flair.

In his prime, Flair could do no wrong. As gifted on the microphone as he was in the ring, Nature Boy was able to elicit any response he chose from the audience. For most of the late 1980s and early 1990s, Flair was the company's lead heel, and more often than not, its champion. He had an uncanny ability to talk up the big game, yet show just enough vulnerability that fans believed that he could lose the belt. And if Ric Flair, this hated playboy, was going to drop the strap, the fans wanted to be there.

In short, he sold tickets. He was WCW's top draw, able to main event with anyone in the company. He was the centerpiece of the promotion, keeping the title around his waist throughout his tenure, the idea being that Flair was more valuable as the hated champion than as the hated challenger.

The same feud awaited every contender to Flair's throne. The babyface, be it Sting, Lex Luger, Ricky Morton, or Dusty Rhodes, would challenge

Flair for the belt. Flair would face his newfound nemesis in some type of nontitle match (be it a singles or a tag), and he would lose cleanly. Therefore, the fans knew that Flair could be beaten. They had seen it with their own eyes. The next step was a title match, which Flair would lose, albeit by count-out or disqualification, so the title did not change hands.

The problem was that although Flair could draw, there were people behind the scenes who did not care for him. Bookers such as Ole Anderson and corporate types such as WCW Vice President Jim Herd often let their personal conflicts with Flair get in the way of doing what was best for business. Such was the case after Flair lost the belt to Sting in 1990.

Fans loved Sting. He was young, energetic, and, above all, seemed to genuinely care about the folks in the stands. Children in the crowd would often spike their hair and paint their faces to look like their hero. The roar of the crowd seemed to motivate the Stinger, and there was a real feeling among fans that he was something special. Flair thought so, too. Behind the scenes, he pushed hard for Sting to be the successor to his throne.

Although Sting was a popular champion, he suffered from a lack of credible challengers. To anyone with a brain, the obvious solution would have been to pit Sting against the guy whom he beat for the belt in a series of rematches. After all, the company had been built around Flair so long that he more often had the belt than not, and fans obviously believed that Flair could once again win the belt. But the powers that be in the promotion, led by Anderson and Herd, were dead set against Flair being the top contender to Sting's belt. Therefore, new challengers had to be found.

This gave a very inexperienced monster by the name of Sid Vicious his first shot at glory, when he was put into a program with Sting leading up to the *Halloween Havoc 1990* pay-per-view. Vicious was a huge man, viewed by many as WCW's version of Hulk Hogan. In some respects, he was superior to Hogan. While not as tall as the Hulkster, his rock-hard physique was much more cut. Although he was by no means an Olympic gymnast, he was also quite agile for a man of his size. Indeed, compared to WWF stiffs like Hogan or Big John Studd, he looked downright nimble. More than anything, though, Sid Vicious just looked like he could kick your ass. Given this set of credentials, it at least made sense that WCW would give the big guy a shot.

What didn't make much sense, however, was how his match with Sting played out. The bout was like any other championship match until Sid lured Sting away from the ring and down the entrance aisle. After vanishing from the fans' view, Sid came staggering back to the ring with Sting in tow. For some reason, however, Sting was suddenly seven inches taller, and at least 50 pounds fatter. Sting collapsed to the mat, no doubt due to this sudden change in his physiology. Sid fell on top of him for the three count, and was handed the world title.

But all was not as it seemed! Suddenly, another Sting bolted from the back and hit Sid with a Stinger Splash (his trademark flying body attack). The referee, the same one who had just awarded Sid the belt, realized that *this* was the real Sting, and that the porky dude in the ring was a fraud, a display of deductive logic that gives him the distinction of being the smartest referee in the history of pro wrestling. Sting went on to win the match and retain the title.

That took care of the real Sting, but who was that pudgy Sting whom Sid had pinned in the ring? It was actually Sid Vicious's running buddy, Barry Windham. Every once in a while, wrestling promotions attempt this kind of thing, and it almost never works. When it does work, it is due to the fact that the impostor looks at least somewhat like the wrestler he is impersonating. The fact that Barry Windham and Sting were both blond male Caucasians probably wouldn't have been enough similarity for most bookers, but it was good enough for Ole Anderson. It wasn't good enough for the fans, though, and the booking for the match accomplished virtually nothing. It didn't make Sting look like a strong champion, it made Sid look like a goof who couldn't win the big one on his own. In fact, following this match, Vicious floundered about the WCW midcard until his contract expired, then headed to the greener pastures of the WWF in an attempt to more directly lay claim to the title "The Next Hulk Hogan."

It wasn't that WCW didn't have talented grapplers. They did. They just had no clue how to use them. Mike Rotundo, for instance, was a superb collegiate wrestler out of Syracuse. He had made a name for himself during the mid-1980s in the WWF, winning the tag belts with Windham (who was, at that time, not masquerading as Sting). When Rotundo got to WCW, how- ever, the company seemed confused as to exactly how to use him. They had a hard time even remembering how to spell his last name, as it cycled from "Rotundo" to "Rotunda" and back on a weekly basis. Arguments en-sued in the back as to whether "Rotunda" was easier to remember than "Rotundo." Finally, after nearly a year of intense feuding, the *A* was retired and the big *O* took over.

Rotundo was given numerous personas during his WCW tenure. He first arrived as part of a heel stable known as the Varsity Club, in which he teamed with former Michigan alum Rick Steiner. The pair would often argue over who was the "captain" of their team, eventually leading to a split and a babyface run for Steiner. Rotundo was excellent in his role, displaying a natural ability to play the part of the bad guy.

So it should come as no shock that WCW turned him babyface. What was shocking, however, was that while they changed his gimmick, they kept his nickname. "Captain" Mike Rotundo was no longer the captain of a football team or a wrestling squad, but rather the captain of a boat! With no explanation whatsoever, Rotundo began wearing sailor's gear to the ring, complete with an anchor emblazoned on his fanny. This led to the formation of Captain Mike's Captain's Crew with other outcasts, such as Big Trucker Norm.

Trucker Norm was an interesting case in his own right. Born Mike Shaw in May of 1957, Norm was a huge man, over six feet tall and tipping the scales past 350 pounds. He learned the trade under the guidance of grizzled veteran Killer Kowalski. Shaw garnered even more knowledge during an early run with Stampede Wrestling in Calgary, Alberta, under the watchful eye of Stu Hart, father of WWF superstars Bret and Owen Hart. He was fairly agile for a man of his size, and he wound up with WCW in the late 1980s.

The original plan was for Norm to be a madman, in the vein of the WWF's George "The Animal" Steele. A story line was concocted that had Norman being discovered in an insane asylum by heel manager Teddy Long. Sadly, the reason why a pro wrestling manager would be frequenting such a location was never explained.

As Norman the Lunatic, Shaw was portrayed as a wild madman. However, because he was under the thumb of Long, he was also often depicted as a sympathetic character. The diminutive manager would berate the big man, keeping him under lock and key — literally. Norman would be brought to the ring strapped to a gurney, wrestle his match, then be locked down again and wheeled to the back. Long carried around a huge gold key that supposedly opened the (apparently gigantic) doors to Norman's former home. The message seemed pretty clear: do as I say, or back to the nuthouse you go.

This naturally led to a split between Long and Norman, with the Lunatic becoming a fan favorite in every sense of the word. When he wasn't coming to the ring throwing teddy bears to the crowd, he was foiling the evil plots of men such as Long. He was beginning to really get over with the gimmick, which, of course, meant that it was time for a change.

Norman the Lunatic then became "Big Trucker" Norm. He was given the name because he supposedly drove a truck for a living. This angle seemed to overlook the fact that Norm was currently employed as a professional wrestler. Perhaps he drove the truck during the day and wrestled by night. Or maybe he drove the ring from town to town. What was certain was that this former crazy man was now driving an 18-wheeler across the highways and byways of America.

According to an interview with Greg Oliver in the *Calgary Sun*, Shaw had heat with head booker Anderson, who, for reasons unknown, didn't care for Norman. Anderson therefore took the character, changed it, and then killed it.

As for Shaw, he ran a wrestling school for a few years before getting a call from New York. Vince McMahon had an idea for a character based on him, an idea that wound up being even more idiotic than that of an oversized truck driver who was discovered in an insane asylum. But we'll come back to that later.

For now, let's get back to Rotundo. Shockingly, he didn't get over as a sea captain, likely due to the fact that folks who own yachts probably don't watch much pro wrestling. The bookers wisely decided to turn Rotundo heel. Unfortunately, they gave him yet another completely different persona, this time in the form of Michael Wallstreet, evil business tycoon.

The character was based almost entirely upon Ted DiBiase's highly successful Million Dollar Man character from the WWF. Both played the part of the nefarious millionaire who would use his wealth to overrun the company. The primary difference was that Wallstreet had a computer genius cohort by the name of Alexandra York in his corner.

The idea was that York would input all the strengths and weaknesses of Wallstreet's opponents into the program, and the computer would print out an exact game plan of how to achieve victory. More often than not, this intricate, detailed strategy would involve Wallstreet grabbing the laptop from York and smacking the opponent in the head. Wallstreet and York analyzed opponents, plotted, schemed, and mapped out careers to championships. They laughed in an evil manner. Yes, they certainly enjoyed a good evil laugh.

Alexandra's computer program was a smash. It worked so well she was able to create a stable of unbeatable wrestlers, the York Foundation. The only problem, of course, was that the wrestlers in the Foundation never won. Rotundo quickly tired of the gimmick and left for the WWF to become evil tax agent Irwin R. Schyster (IRS, get it?). Terry Taylor, fresh from being a rooster in the WWF, was brought in to save the situation, but eventually he just wound up adding another failed gimmick to his resumé as the "Computerized Man of the '90s," Terrance Taylor. Finally, the plug was yanked on this experiment, and the Radio Shack special went back to doing the only thing it was really suited to do—playing "Hunt the Wumpus."

Another tried-and-true crutch in pro wrestling story lines is the "dueling musical styles" angle, and WCW played this card as well. Rap versus country, rap versus rock, rock versus classical, country versus rock; every variation has been tried. There was, for example, "Rapmaster" P.N. News, a 400-pound tub of goo from the vaguely mean streets of a town whose name is never mentioned, against Johnny B. Badd, whose greatest attribute, according to his entrance music, was that he looked just like Little Richard.

He did, too. Badd was the brainchild of booker Dusty Rhodes, played to perfection by former boxer Marc Mero. It was almost shocking how much Mero, with the aid of a ton of makeup, was the spitting image of the freakish entertainer from Macon, Georgia. Of course, this being wrestling, the whole ordeal was taken way over the top, and Mero was instructed to act as tutti-frutti as possible. In time, his performances included all manner of feminism, including feathered boas and little plastic lips he would place on his fallen adversaries. Eventually, a confetti popgun, dubbed the "Badd Blaster," also found its way into wrestling rings.

This was all a shame, too, because in his prime Mero was a hell of a worker. Over time, he fought valiantly to eliminate the cartoonish aspects of the persona. His in-ring work became the focus of his routine, and fans took notice. Still, he was haunted throughout his WCW tenure by being known as "that Little Richard guy." Sad, really, because who in their right mind would think that dressing a guy up as a 1950s rock legend would create a stir?

Probably the same brain surgeons who thought there should be a pair of wrestlers who had hunchbacks. You have to love the logic: "They can't be beat, because when you pin one of their shoulders to the mat, the other one will be up! It will be great!" Weebles wobble but they can't be pinned, so to speak.

Hailing from Notre Dame, the fabulous Hunchbacks would carry a bell to the ring. Amazingly, it was a gimmick that even Ole Anderson found too absurd to promote. But Jim Herd, who came up with the idea, was nothing if not persistent, and he altered the gimmick slightly in order for Anderson to finally give it the green light. Herd relented on the humps but continued to claim that wrestlers who brought bells out to the ring would be an instant sensation. And thus the Ding Dongs were born.

Stop and think about this for a moment: the *vice president* of the company thought a tag team known as the *Ding Dongs* would make money.

The Dongs came to the ring wearing bright-orange masks and outfits bedecked in bells. They brought a huge bell to the ring with them that they rang during the *entire match* to the delight of . . . well . . . no one. Strange, isn't it? You'd think that a bell clanging for ten minutes straight would be wildly entertaining. During their first-ever match, at *Clash of the Champions IX*, they were booed out of the building and were lucky to escape with their lives. Even Herd finally realized what a horrible idea this was, and the Ding Dongs were silenced forever.

It was often the case that WCW wished to tap into the children's market, which the WWF had proven was profitable. The Ding Dongs were one such attempt to cater to a younger audience, but there were many others as well. Big Josh, for example, was a friendly lumberjack who hailed from the none-too-specific hometown of "the woods." During his debut, WCW actually brought in bears that danced about the stage as Josh made his entrance. Because, as everyone knows, kids love dancing bears.

Well, maybe not, but they definitely love superheroes. Surely the kids in the audience would take to a wall-crawling champion of justice who fired webs from his wrists. And so, longtime journeyman Brad Armstrong donned a costume that looked suspiciously like a Spider-Man outfit, albeit in the wrong colors. But this wasn't Spider-Man — it was Arachniman. Was he strong? Listen, bub! He had radioactive blood!

Marvel Comics didn't take too kindly to this blatant theft and served WCW with a cease and desist order mere weeks after Arachniman's debut. WCW responded by giving Armstrong yet another lame gimmick in the form of the Candyman, for which poor Brad wore candy-cane-striped tights to the ring and threw sweets to the children in the crowd. Likely due to the fact that he didn't come out to the Sammy Davis classic of the same name, this didn't get over either.

The Dynamic Dudes was another idea that was designed to appeal to the younger set. Johnny Ace and Shane Douglas were a new team that WCW designated as beach bums, complete with brightly colored beach outfits. Although they were supposedly from the beach, they would often carry skateboards rather than surfboards to the ring. Of course, they never actually rode the skateboards, so it was obvious to fans that the Dudes would have no clue what to do with the props they carried to the ring. Maybe if they had beaten their opponents over the heads with the skateboards they'd have gotten over, but, sadly, this wasn't meant to be. After the Dudes did a short stint on their own, WCW management decided that pairing the floundering duo with loudmouth manager Jim Cornette would be a good idea. Cornette was treading water as well, as the bookers seemed to have no idea what to do with his flagship tag team, the Midnight Express.

The Express was unquestionably one of the greatest teams of the day. The duo, which consisted of Bobby Eaton and Stan Lane, took the concept of tag team wrestling to new heights, with complicated double-team maneuvers that looked to cripple their opponents. Cornette, meanwhile, would have his trusty tennis racket at hand, ready to interfere when the referee's back was turned. Fans hated the Express but would pay good money to see them in hopes that they would be there when they got their eventual comeuppance.

By early 1990, however, their long feud with the rival Rock & Roll Express was played out. Since there was really no one else on the face side of things who would pose a viable challenge, the Express were turned baby-face, thus negating all the double-team moves that formerly infuriated fans. Cornette was especially neutered by the move; his loudmouth boasts were something fans loved to hate.

A master plan came about involving the Dudes and the Express, wherein Cornette would manage both teams. The two teams began to interfere in each other's matches as they vied for the lion's share of Cornette's attention. Eventually, a match between the two was signed, and going in, it appeared as though Cornette was soundly behind the surfer boys. As the match reached its conclusion, however, Cornette shockingly cracked Douglas over the head with his racket, which should have ensured the Dudes a sympathetic reaction from the crowd. The logic was that Cornette and the Mid-nights would return to being hated by the fans for doing something so underhanded.

All good in theory, but in real life the fans erupted as though Cornette had just found the cure for cancer. The Dudes experiment was killed off entirely after this reaction, and the Express continued to flounder until Lane and Cornette took off to build their own promotion, Smoky Mountain Wrestling. Eaton hung around WCW until the bitter end. Douglas bounced from promotion to promotion, burning bridges along the way. Ace headed to Japan to become a major star, which he was somehow able to do without the aid of a skateboard.

Mark Hildreth, though, was never quite that fortunate. He was branded for life when he became "Heavy Metal" Van Hammer. He was a huge man who had never displayed an ability to elicit a crowd response, but on the plus side, he was big and muscular. On this basis alone, WCW felt that he had a chance of wowing the pimply-faced girls in the audience. Therefore, they gave him a flying-V guitar and told him to commence headbanging. An elaborate music video was created hyping his debut at *Clash of the Champions XVI*, and the announce crew treated his entrance into the promotion as though a lost member of Led Zeppelin had just been discovered.

His debut match left a lot of fans wondering what all the fuss was about. It wasn't so much that his in-ring performance was horrible. Well, that's not quite true; he really, really sucked. The larger issue, though, seemed to be that this guy who was supposedly a rock star of *Spinal Tap* proportions obviously had no clue how to play a guitar. Sure, he knew how to bang his head, but it was clear to fans he was nothing more than a poseur.

While Hammer was a wrestler posing as a rock star, Jorge Gonzalez had a hard enough time just posing as a wrestler. Gonzalez, a 7'7" Argentinean looking for work after a failed career with the NBA's Atlanta Hawks, was brought in and immediately thrown into the main event scene. Since Turner owned both the Hawks and WCW, there was some discussion between the organizations that maybe Gonzalez could make it in wrestling. The basketball team felt that wrestling could work for him, since his knees wouldn't be under the stress that had cut short his NBA career. Those on the wrestling side of things simply saw this huge man, a real freak of nature, and thought it was worth a shot.

Gonzalez entered WCW amidst much fanfare. Promos built up his impending arrival as El Gigante, which translates to "The Giant." Some WCW commentators, however, had a hard time pronouncing this and instead called him "El Egante," which means "elegant." This was pretty ironic, because "elegant" would be the last word anyone would use to describe Gonzalez, unless his custom-made aluminum-foil headband could somehow be construed as classy. This headgear was apparently designed to reflect his heritage, inasmuch as aluminum foil can represent a country. WCW promoters hoped that viewers would be able to connect with this new giant as they had with the legendary Andre the Giant years before. WCW found out that capturing lightning twice is difficult, no matter what the size of the bottle.

For starters, Gonzalez spoke almost no English whatsoever. While Andre was never the most well-spoken of wrestlers, his broken English was miles ahead of what Gonzalez had to offer. Andre was not only tall, but large as well. He was built like a tank, with a tremendous torso that dwarfed even his largest opponents. Gonzalez was plenty tall, but his slender frame didn't inspire a sense of awe in fans. He didn't look like a giant. He just looked like an out-of-work basketball player.

The biggest difference between Andre and Gonzalez, though, was what they did inside the ring. Andre would never be mistaken for a scientific master of the mat, but he understood how to use his bulk to create a match that people wanted to watch. He knew just how to attack his opponents so that it would be believable, but not deadly. He also knew how to sell (act injured), and when to make his comeback for maximum impact.

Gonzalez knew none of this. Rushed into the ring by greedy promoters, he had no more than a few weeks' worth of training prior to his in-ring debut. He fumbled about the ring, failing to execute even the most basic of maneuvers with any believability at all. Even Ric Flair, a magician in the ring, had a hard time getting a good match out of him. Gonzalez was, arguably, the worst wrestler in recorded history.

The failure of El Gigante did little to stop the import of more former professional athletes to WCW rings. Bill Kazmaier was brought into the company as the "World's Strongest Man." Take this to the bank: anytime you hear those three words strung together to promote a wrestler, he will fail. Promoters seem to love legitimate athletes, guys who have achieved fame in other sporting arenas. And while it would seem that two related fields — such as power lifting and wrestling — would be a natural match, it almost never works out.

Much like Ted Arcidi in the mid-'80s WWF, Kazmaier was a legitimate weight lifting phenomenon. Kazmaier was a phenomenal specimen, able to bench-press 650 pounds, and at 6'3" and 350 pounds, he looked more like a pro wrestler than Arcidi had. He was so well built, in fact, that several researchers did studies on him, just to see what the real limitations of human strength are.

Of course, all of this meant nothing in a pro wrestling ring. Kazmaier had no real fire, and fans had a hard time relating to the guy. Having him carry a big globe on his back (presumably to emphasize the fact that he was the *world's* strongest man) did little to get the fans off their seats.

As laughable as all these gimmicks were, though, none could compare to the mighty and powerful Oz.

Fans who have only recently caught the wrestling bug know Kevin Nash as either "Big Sexy" or the character that brought him to the forefront of the wrestling scene, Diesel. Standing almost seven feet tall, and with a massive upper body that hides his chicken legs, there is no question why promoters have repeatedly given Nash opportunity after opportunity. He is certainly an impressive physical specimen. WCW surely felt that Nash was money in the bank when he walked through their front door. So much so, in fact, that they decided to create a pet project around him.

In the mid-'80s, Ted Turner purchased the television rights to over 3,000 films in the MGM library, including *The Wizard of Oz*, for around $1 billion. The idea of cross-promotion was either suggested or shoved down the throats of those in charge of the wrestling arm of the Turner empire. And what better way to encourage wrestling fans to view classic movie reruns than by creating a character based on the best-known wizard this side of Kansas?

And so Kevin Nash became Oz, powerful sorcerer overlord of the wrestling ring. During his initial appearances, he had the most elaborate entrance devised to that point in wrestling, employing all manner of lighting and a fog machine to enhance his eerie aura. Coming toward his giant castle were Dorothy, Tin Man, Cowardly Lion, and the Scarecrow. They were led by an impish man in a horrible mask, dubbed the Wizard, who was carrying a monkey, all the while chanting, "Welcome to Oz! Welcome to Oz!"

The idea was that all of this would not only make fans long to see more Oz matches, but also convince them to stick around for repeated viewings of *The Wizard of Oz* on the Superstation. Shockingly, this did not happen. Despite the incredible buildup and insane cost to build the set for his entrance, let alone the expense of renting a monkey, the entire Oz gimmick was killed off in a manner of weeks.

And no, they didn't drop a house on Kevin Nash.

Unfortunately.

No, Kevin Nash lived, and even kept his job as a pro wrestler, likely due to the fact that he was very tall and a funny guy behind the scenes. He was repackaged as Vinnie Vegas, a two-bit thug from Nevada. This gimmick lasted slightly longer than Oz, but it didn't get over with fans any better, and Nash was eventually released from his contract in 1993. He wound up in the WWF, became Diesel, and damn near bankrupted the company during his reign as champion.

WCW had an overabundance of characters in its stable that fans either hated or, worse, simply didn't care about. Which brings us back to where we started: Sting as champ, with no one as a legitimate contender. No one, of course, except Ric Flair, whom Ole Anderson and Jim Herd didn't like.

So Anderson came up with a unique solution to the problem. If there was no one in the promotion he wanted to push as the number-one contender, then by God he would create someone. And thus the Black Scorpion was born.

The Scorpion was to be Sting's top nemesis. Shrouded in mystery for the first several months of his WCW existence, he never once performed in front of a live crowd, appearing instead in a series of vignettes in which he alluded to his shared past with Sting. With his face veiled in darkness and his voice electronically distorted, he would murmur such things as, "California . . . in '87," and then threaten that while others were simply after Sting's title, he was out to kill him. Yes, kill him, as in R.I.P., DEAD. That's a pretty deep hatred.

As if all this mystery weren't enough, Scorpion claimed to have mystical powers of the black magic variety. During one of Scorpion's first live appearances, he grabbed a "member of the audience" from the crowd. Should you ever see such a thing happen at a live event, the first thing that should pop into your head is "PLANT!" A *plant* is someone the promotion sticks in the crowd for story line advancement. Grabbing a real person out of the crowd is a lawsuit waiting to happen, and even WCW wasn't dumb enough to do that.

Especially not with the vile plot the Scorpion was about to unleash. The Scorpion placed a small box around the man's head, then proceeded to spin it like a top. As fans sat in quiet awe at the mighty Scorpion's mystical powers, he took the man and threw him into a strategically placed cage. Scorpion spouted some gibberish about destroying Sting and then pulled back his cape. TA-DA! The fan had turned into a tiger! Yes, a tiger, just like you would see at the zoo. If this was supposed to have scared Sting, then it's not clear why WCW didn't simply send David Copperfield after him.

Behind the scenes, things really were starting to resemble a zoo. As WCW was pushing the Scorpion and his two-bit Blackstone act to the moon, they forgot to take care of one rather important detail: figuring out exactly who the Scorpion was. They had absolutely no idea who would play the part when the inevitable unmasking was to occur. The original plan was to reveal a little-known wrestler by the name of Angel of Death under the hood, as he had teamed with Sting early in his career and it would actually have made sense. The problem was that no one, aside from the most hardcore of fans, would have any clue who he was. This was too much for even Herd to handle, and he demanded a solution as *Starrcade 1990*, WCW's biggest show of the year, was fast approaching, with Sting vs. Black Scorpion at the top of the card.

At the show, the crowd sat in stunned silence as the Black Scorpion made his entrance. But then another Black Scorpion made his entrance, followed by two more. Finally, a giant *spaceship* came down from the ceiling, dropping off the last, and presumably the "real," Black Scorpion on the runway. God knows how much WCW spent on the production of the Scorpion's entrance alone, but had they forgone this elaborate entrance, they likely would have had enough to pay a well-known wrestler to appear under the mask and have the angle make at least *some* sense.

Instead, though, fans got a spaceship, a spaceship that was never seen again.

Sting and the Scorpion proceeded to have an entertaining match that seemed strangely familiar. At the end of the match, all the Scorpions attacked Sting, but they were run off by various babyfaces from the locker room. Finally, Sting yanked the mask off the "real" Scorpion to reveal none other than . . . Ric Flair.

Yes, Ric Flair. The guy the promotion didn't want to push as the number-one contender. The guy Ole Anderson and Jim Herd had banished to the midcard. With no other options, Anderson had turned to Flair to help him out of the mess he had created. Flair had agreed to become the Scorpion in exchange for one small favor: he would soon thereafter defeat Sting and get one more run with the belt. Herd was livid about the entire situation, and fired Anderson immediately following this. And while Flair was overjoyed that he was once again world champion, his euphoria would be short lived.

He was about to join Ole in the unemployment line.

The Boat Goes Boom

Not long after the Black Scorpion fiasco, Jim Herd gave Ric Flair the boot. Herd's logic was solid; buy rates and attendance were dropping steadily, and he took that to mean that fans were tired of Flair, likely due to his age. This left WCW in a tricky predicament, as the company had been built around Flair for so long that it was almost synonymous with the Nature Boy. As the struggle to find its identity intensified, as the promotion tried various gimmicks, angles, and matches to find its niche. More often than not, it failed. Failed spectacularly, in fact, and the results were usually hilarious, if unintentionally so.

A perfect example of their ineptitude was during 1991's *Halloween Havoc* pay-per-view. In an attempt to build fan interest, a cage match was booked for the show and hyped for months in advance. All of the top WCW stars were to be in the match: Scott Hall, Sting, Cactus Jack, Big Van Vader, and the Steiners were all to wage war inside the cage. There would be no winners—only survivors. Since the match was to be held at *Halloween Havoc*, WCW decided to play on the seasonal theme. The announcers and some of the wrestlers themselves played dress-up, the highlight being Eric Bischoff appearing as a vampire, lovingly referred to by fans the world over as Count Fagula.

They also decided to transform the cage into a "Chamber of Horrors." No one had ever seen such a cage or heard of such a match, so fans were confused as to what to expect. WCW wasn't exactly forthright in providing them with details, either, likely due to the fact that they themselves were unsure of exactly what they were going to do.

The night of the show, an elaborate set was revealed from which the wrestlers emerged. Well, that's not quite true. The set actually consisted of a sheet with a haunted house painted on it, used as a backdrop, and a bunch of Styrofoam headstones that littered the entrance ramp, each with a cornball epitaph like, "Here lies Fred. A big rock fell on his head." In short, it appeared as though the Turner folks had stolen a set from a third-grade production of *The Legend of Sleepy Hollow*.

But the cage itself was a sight to behold! Whereas most cages in wrestling butt up next to the ring, this one was much larger, allowing the combatants to move around outside the ring, but still inside the cage. It even had a roof, unheard of at the time. Inside the cage were caskets, shrunken heads, and other assorted "weapons of torture." And midway through the match, an electric chair would descend from the ceiling into the ring.

Reread that last line, please. Yes, there was an *electric chair* in the ring. But this wasn't just any old run-of-the-mill electric chair, like you would find in a maximum-security prison. Oh no. It was the dreaded "Chair of Torture!" The object of said match was to put your opponent in the electric ch—— . . . er . . . "Chair of Torture," and then to throw the "Fatal Lever," which hung inside the cage, complete with a helpful on/off switch. Throwing the lever would, according to the WCW announce crew, render the opponent helpless.

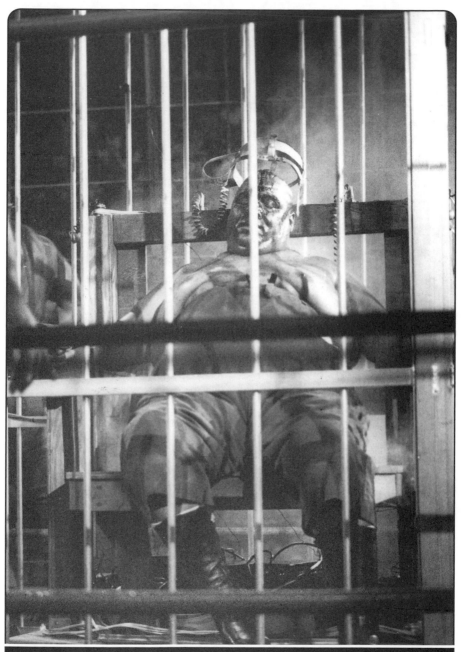

Abdullah the Butcher sizzles like a cheap steak in the Chair of Torture.

The match progressed very, very slowly. There was very little action aside from one notable incident: the Fatal Lever actually dropped into the on position. Shockingly (or perhaps not, pun fully intended), nothing happened. Cactus Jack scurried up the cage and attempted to put the lever back into its proper position quietly, but, of course, it was all captured on camera for the fans at home. The announcers didn't even attempt to explain the mishap.

Finally, Rick Steiner was able to secure Abdullah the Butcher into the chair, and Cactus, thinking that it was Steiner in the chair, threw the lever. A pyrotechnic show followed as Abby sat in the chair, jiggling about in a vain effort to convince fans that he was being fried. An EMT unit, with faces all painted white so as to appear, well, scary, then arrived to haul the carcass out of the ring.

As horrible as all this sounds, it actually got worse as the year progressed, leading up to the year's biggest event, "the granddaddy of them all," *Starrcade*. For the 1991 version of the event, booker Dusty Rhodes came up with a novel idea: a tournament in which tag teams were formed by random draws, with winning teams heading to a double-ring battle royal at the end of the evening. This could indeed have been a very intriguing concept, save for one small matter: the drawing really *was* random.

It made little sense to anyone, except maybe Dusty himself, why a company that promoted scripted wrestling matches would just throw a foursome out into the ring to compete — and not just once, but for the duration of the show, the biggest show of the year! The card was a big mess, as the few veterans on the show who were able to do a match on the fly were paired up with either younger workers or wrestlers with incom-

patible styles. The ending of the evening, with longtime favorite Sting ous
ting hated champion Lex Luger, was scripted, but it did little to appease
most fans' displeasure with the show.

Fans were no more pleased when a group of gunslingers began to
devour valuable TV time during WCW broadcasts. The trio, known as the
Desperados, consisted of longtime journeyman Black Bart, longtime journeyman Dutch Mantell, and deaf, dumb, and half-blind journeyman Dead
Eye Dick. Of course, Dick wasn't really deaf or blind, but for some reason
the masterminds at WCW thought this would add to his persona.

The Desperados never kicked any ass nor took any names. Shockingly,
they never even wrestled! They simply bumbled around Old West movie
sets in a vain attempt to locate fellow cowboy wrestler Stan Hansen. But
these buffoons never ran into Hansen because, after seeing the initial skits,
Hansen wanted nothing to do with it.

Amazingly, things started getting better in early 1992, as the Dangerous
Alliance hit the scene, led by future ECW creator Paul Heyman (aka Paul
E. Dangerously) and featuring a young unknown by the name of Steve Austin.
Additionally, WCW imported several Japanese stars, improving match
quality by leaps and bounds.

But hey, a book entitled *WrestleCrap* isn't about the great moments in
wrestling; it's about the worst. And fortunately for you, dear reader, WCW
reverted back to its usual inept self by Halloween of 1992.

Hoping, no doubt, to surpass its *Havoc* offering of the previous year,
WCW threw a bunch of money at one of the WWF's biggest former stars,
Jake "The Snake" Roberts, and brought him into the fold. Roberts was last
seen in the WWF, you'll recall, as the Ultimate Warrior's evil guru. After

Warrior packed up and left, Jake was used as cannon fodder for the freshly turned babyface Undertaker. He was still a huge draw for the Federation until personal demons came a-haunting.

A note to the uninitiated: whenever people in the wrestling business speak of "personal demons," they are referring either to domestic violence or substance abuse, usually the latter. However, it sounds much nicer to say Jake was "confronting his demons" than to say Jake was "stoned out of his mind." That's probably because the "demons" line is so vague that no one could sue over it. So, let us simply agree that Jake had issues with his personal demons, and then nod, wink, smile, and move on.

Roberts was being brought in to feud with WCW's hottest star, Sting. Since WCW was paying Roberts big bucks, they wanted to make sure that the move paid off, and they wisely decided to promote the hell out of their upcoming pay-per-view showdown at *Halloween Havoc '92*. They did so by turning the match into a "Spin the Wheel, Make the Deal" encounter.

Even longtime fans of the pseudo-sport of pro wrestling were scratching their heads, attempting to figure out what the hell a "Spin the Wheel, Make the Deal" match was. No one had ever heard of such a thing. The truth was that WCW was simply inventing a match and hoping that it would generate interest, much as they had with the previous year's "Chamber of Horrors." What's that old saying about those who ignore history being doomed to repeat it?

In order to further entice buys for the show, WCW commissioned a film crew and prepared to make a minimovie documenting the bad blood between Sting and Jake the Snake. This would also allow WCW to clue fans into the psychology of the match. The production values for the segment were actually far beyond any that wrestling had seen at the time — it really did look like a movie. A horribly written and acted B-grade movie, but a movie nonetheless.

The segment took place in a seedy bar. The seediness of said bar was indicated by its seedy patrons—countless thugs, hoodlums, goons, and toughs. There was also a guy in a Hannibal Lecter mask, and several "women of the night." To top it all off, there was a very evil—and undeniably seedy—midget by the name of Cheatum, bedecked with an eye patch. You can talk seedy all you want, but unless you've got a one-eyed midget named Cheatum, you're really just talking out of your ass.

The centerpiece of the bar was a big spiky wheel, complete with dueling, smoke-snorting snake statues. Of course, it wouldn't have been much of a bar without wrestling's answer to Otis, and the star of the show, Jake Roberts himself. A dominatrix (whom longtime fans would recognize as former Dangerous Alliance cohort Madusa Micelli) began to fondle the penis-shaped lever as the group of no-goodniks chanted "Spin the Wheel, Make the Deal!"

Just as the party started to get rocking, the decidedly unseedy Sting showed up in a billow of fog, causing the gang to cower at his very presence. Roberts, though, was unshaken. Sting headed straight for Jake as the tough guys parted like the Red Sea. The two traded wooden dialogue, with such classic lines as, "You think I'm afraid of some wheel? You think I'm afraid of you?" and Cheatum taunted Sting at every turn. The crowd "oohed" and "aahed," their heads turning back and forth as though they were following a tennis match.

And thus, fans discovered that "Spin the Wheel, Make the Deal" didn't refer to a match at all, but rather to an actual, physical wheel. The type of match Roberts and Sting would fight would be determined by a spin of the wheel. Would it be a cage match? A scaffold match? A death match? A lumberjack match?

Finally, Sting declared that he had had enough and went up to spin the wheel. As the wheel began to spin, Roberts and Sting engaged in a staredown. Just as they were about to "make the deal" and determine what type of match they would have, laser beams came out of their eyes toward each other, and everything exploded.

Thankfully, both men recovered from the explosion in time to meet up for the match at *Halloween Havoc '92*. Early in the show, Sting was able to spin the wheel without the distraction of Jake's eyeball lasers, and the match was made: a Coal Miner's Glove match. After all, why have a cage match when you can have two men fighting over a mitten?

If you've never heard of a Coal Miner's Glove match, you're not alone. It was basically just a variation on the old wrestling standard "Item on a Pole" match, only in this case, said item was a glove with some indistinct piece of metal wrapped around it. This kind of match tends to be very boring, with the focus being on who can climb up a pole the fastest. Enthralling, no? In this case, the match ended when the Stinger successfully retrieved the glove and hit Jake in the face with it. Jake was beaten, but he had a backup plan. He unleashed his deadly venomous cobra at Sting, but the snake attacked Roberts instead, biting him in the jaw.

At least, that was what was supposed to happen.

In reality, Jake couldn't get the snake to bite him, so he just sort of held it up to his face and writhed about in mock pain. At one point, Jake was so mad at the snake that he hit it on the head a couple of times. The snake responded by just kind of flailing about stupidly, and Roberts kept holding its head against his face in a vain attempt to get the snake to latch onto him as the show ended.

While the setup and the match itself were nothing to write home about, the show did an incredible buy rate for WCW. It was one of their biggest pay-per-views of all time, holding the record for most buys for many, many years. A Sting-Jake rematch should have been a natural.

Except for the fact that Jake began facing his "personal demons" again, making *Halloween Havoc* Jake's first — and last — WCW pay-per-view.

With Roberts gone, Sting, still the company's top babyface whether he had the belt or not, was left without a feud. He bounced around the midcard, facing adversaries such as Rick Rude before settling in for a feud with the behemoth known as Big Van Vader.

Vader was a huge man from the Colorado Rockies (the mountains, not the baseball team). But unlike most big men of that time, he was actually quite agile as well, able to perform moonsaults (backflips) from the top rope with ease. His in-ring performance was vicious — he looked like the most brutal man alive, and he was actually booked as such, winning the WCW world title in late 1992 and holding it for most of 1993. He even had a decent look, complete with a huge metallic helmet that spewed steam upon his command. He was a damn scary dude.

So it was the perfect scenario: the young, popular challenger against the brutal and hated champion. The two were to face off at *SuperBrawl III*, scheduled for February 21, 1993, in Asheville, North Carolina. Nothing else was needed, as the rivalry was so natural.

Leave it to WCW, then, to film an elaborate minimovie featuring a mysterious letter, a helicopter ride, a secret mountain lair named after greasy, miniscule hamburgers, and the return of Cheatum, the evil one-eyed midget. The movie was *The White Castle of Fear*.

Now, it's a generally accepted fact that there's nothing quite as bone-chilling as the prospect of spending time at the local White Castle. Yes, the food is tasty and all, and we all have to have an "Around the World" (that's a White Castle burger, a fish sandwich, a chicken sandwich, a small fries, and a small onion chip with a large Coke) at least once a year. But is it really worth sitting on the commode for the rest of the day?

But wait! Vader's White Castle wasn't a restaurant at all! It was really a *castle*. And it was really *scary*. Or at least that's what WCW would have you believe. In the minimovie, Sting was sent a mysterious invitation from Vader, who asked him to come to a pre-*SuperBrawl* party at his White Castle of Fear. Despite having reservations that this could be, on an off chance, just possibly a trap of some sort, Sting chartered a helicopter to fly him out to the Rocky Mountains, despite having absolutely no idea where the White Castle of Fear actually was. Fortunately, about five minutes into his flight, the pilot spotted Vader's lair, although it was never actually shown on screen.

Sting entered the castle and found a table laid out with an elaborate feast — the centerpiece of which was Vader's steam-spewing helmet in place of the pig with an apple in its mouth. No delicious tiny hamburgers, mind you, but a decent buffet nonetheless. Folks can say what they will about Vader, but he was kind enough to cater for his guests, which included a harem of harlots who appeared to be there for no other reason than to eat fruit and hit on Sting. Our old pal Cheatum was there as well, emphatically imploring Sting to "Play the game! Play the game!" Sting noted that there was something familiar about all this. And indeed there was — it all sucked.

Finally, Vader appeared and began taunting Sting and generally just being a mean, nasty, rotten individual. He made all kinds of grunting and screaming noises, eventually becoming so loud that a mirror shattered in his presence. You've got to be pretty loud to shatter a mirror, you know.

Maybe he should have been a villain in a Hulk Hogan movie. More inane dialogue followed, with Sting stating that the White Castle was a nice place, befitting of Vader's cold personality. Finally, Vader cleared the table, and both men were ready to go to war.

A *tug-of-war*, that is! Both men grabbed opposite ends of a leather strap and proceeded to yank back and forth. Vader's gang of hooligans was cheering him on when suddenly . . . the table burst into flames! Sting was being pulled closer and closer to the flame when even more suddenly . . . everything exploded. Sound familiar? Man, those WCW cats, they sure liked their explosions.

Vader and Sting went on to have a barbaric strap match, delighting fans as Sting pulled out a hard-fought victory. Both men were generating all kinds of interest, so the promotion decided that it was time to bring more folks into the fray to generate more main-event talent. The two men they had in mind for the push were Sid Vicious and Davey Boy Smith, the British Bulldog.

Smith was a WWF cast-off. Formerly one-half of the British Bulldogs tag team with the Dynamite Kid, Smith was well known not only in the United States, but in England and Japan as well. WCW figured they could use Smith to generate interest in their product worldwide and signed him to a contract many times larger than he'd had in the Federation. After having him win a few squash matches on WCW television, WCW was ready to go the next step with him.

Vicious had also just left the WWF, after a *Wrestlemania VIII* main event with Hulk Hogan. Vicious had problems staying in one place, as he was highly unstable outside the ring. That didn't matter to the fans, though; all they knew was that he was tall, lean, and sported an incredibly muscular physique that left them in awe. He wasn't much of a wrestler, but his in-ring performance didn't really matter. He had the look. People were willing to pay money to see him in the ring, even if all he ever really did was just punch and kick his opponent.

WCW aligned Smith with Sting. It was a natural fit, and fans fed off their energy. In the meantime, they had Vicious pair up with Vader. Both men used brutal power bombs as their finishers, so WCW tagged them with the clever "Masters of the Power Bomb" moniker. They were given dual managers, in the form of Harley Race and Col. Robert Parker. The two teams were destined to meet at *Beach Blast* in the summer of 1993.

Beach Blast was an interesting name for a pay-per-view. It made perfect sense in that it took place in the middle of summer, but it rarely took place on a beach. In fact, it rarely took place anywhere *near* a beach. In 1993, however, WCW made sure to emphasize the "blast" part of the title, thanks to yet another minimovie (would they never learn?) featuring Sting, Davey, and the Masters of the Power Bomb.

And, of course, Cheatum, the evil one-eyed midget.

The movie began with Race and Parker requesting that Sting and Davey Boy attend a press conference they were holding to announce the formation of the Masters of the Powerbomb. Sting and Davey Boy were unable to attend, however, as they had already committed to other plans. TheMasters had their press conference anyway, and they gave Sting and Davey a warning: retire or be destroyed.

It turned out that Davey and Sting were actually playing volleyball with underprivileged youths on a remote island. Upon learning this, Race, Parker, Vader, Sid, and Cheatum commissioned a war boat and left to seek out the island, which was "somewhere in the Gulf of Mexico." Fortunately, they were able to find it within a few minutes. After all, it's not like the Gulf of Mexico is *big* or anything, right? They came ashore wearing their wrestling outfits, save for Sid, who was wearing flip-flops instead of boots. It was a good look for him.

Cheatum had other plans in mind. Wearing a snorkel and a shark fin, he swam across the bay and planted a bomb on Sting's boat, with the theme from *Jaws* playing in the background.

Before continuing, it may be in your best interest, dear reader, to stop and ponder this. Picture it in your mind's eye. An evil one-eyed midget named Cheatum swam across the Gulf of Mexico wearing a shark fin on his back and then planted a bomb on a boat. Think about that. Let that sink in.

Now. Wouldn't *you* want to buy a wrestling show after seeing this?

Back to the "story," such as it was. The Masters confronted Sting and Davey in front of the kids, as horrible Western music, likely lifted from one of Turner's countless cowboy flicks, warbled in the background. Parker offered Sting and Davey two tickets to the retirement home of their choice. The fan favorites considered this offer, which made the underprivileged youths sad. Then they decided instead to fight, which made the underprivileged youths happy. Furious at being rebuffed, Parker warned the heroes to enjoy their stay, since it would be a long one. The heels laughed maniacally, and walked off. What could it all mean?

With the bad guys gone, Sting and Davey went back to playing volleyball. A small girl, however, pulled Sting aside to warn him about a funny little man who had been hanging around his boat. Unaware of the nefarious Cheatum's actions, Sting didn't know that his boat was about to EXPLODE! Davey Boy stayed behind to learn more, while Sting headed to the scene of the imminent crime. Finally, Smith ran down the beach, jumped twenty feet into the air, and grabbed Sting as the boat detonated. The children thought the duo was dead, which made them sad. But then the duo resurfaced, alive and well, which made them happy.

While it is unknown how the duo made it off the island, it is known that they made it to their showdown with Vader and Sid at *Beach Blast*, in a boring match that made everyone who viewed it sad. This left the upper card again in need of reshuffling, as neither Sting nor Davey Boy were getting the reaction and buy rates that WCW wanted. They then looked inside the company to find a most unlikely solution to the problem: Cactus Jack.

Jack, who would go on to greater heights as Mankind, Dude Love, and by his real name, Mick Foley, was something very different for WCW. He wasn't handsome, he wasn't tall, he wasn't muscular, and he didn't have a good physique. But there was one thing he could do as well as anyone in the company, and that was take enormous sums of punishment.

Which is exactly what Vader dealt out. Although it is generally accepted that professional wrestling is scripted, this doesn't mean that injuries don't occur. They do, constantly. Some wrestlers are also more delicate than others in their performance, making sure not to hurt anyone as they work a match. Others are what insiders refer to as "stiff," meaning that they don't pull their punches as much as they perhaps should. And no one in the business was as stiff as Vader.

That's why his feud with Cactus was a dream. Vader could be as stiff as he wanted; Jack could take it. They had brutal matches, with two incidents being the most famous. The first occurred on WCW's nationally televised show, *WCW Saturday Night*. Vader and Jack were in the midst of one of their typically barbaric affairs when they ventured outside the ring. Vader lifted Jack high into the air and then slammed his back and neck onto the concrete floor. Jack passed out from the pain, as everyone, including Vader, looked on with great concern.

The other instance is even more famous. While on a tour of Germany, Vader tangled Jack in the ropes and began to pummel him. As Jack struggled to free himself, he lost a good portion of his ear. Yes, as unbelievable as it may seem, he actually lost his ear. With such a ferocious history, it seemed as though a meeting between the two needed no more buildup. WCW could just let the two loose in the ring.

Of course, they didn't do that, deciding instead to film a series of vignettes entitled "Lost in Cleveland," making what should have been the highlight of Mick Foley's career into one of his worst angles ever. The vignettes featured a bogus news reporter named Catherine White. White was attempting to hunt down Cactus Jack, who no one had seen since the *Saturday Night* match with Vader. White was able to track Jack down somewhere in Cleveland, where he had befriended a group of homeless people. One of the homeless folks was a con artist by the name of Swampy, who led the daffy reporter to Jack's secret hideout.

As she ventured to speak with Jack, she noticed something was awry. He wasn't talking about his many battles in the ring, but rather discussing ports he had visited and storms he had survived at sea. Indeed, he was preaching to his little group about his life at sea. Now, let it be known that neither the character Cactus Jack or the man Mick Foley had any such background. So why was he talking such nonsense? Because he had amnesia, of course!

He would wax philosophical to his peers: "And so I've lived most of my life on the sea, and I've learned that life on land is very much the same. Oh, some would say, 'No, Matey, it's very different. Out there on the ocean your horizons are unlimited, while here on land you can see only as far as the next rise.' And while it's true that from a crow's nest you can see farther than most of us will ever see, from a clear horizon every point looks the same."

Amnesia or no, Cactus was still a babyface. In fact, he was able to convince Swampy that he was better off working for a living than drinking. He even repaired little children's bicycles, telling one child, "Here you go, Jenny — she's an old vessel but she's seaworthy again. Should be clear sailing on that paper route of yours."

White decided, for whatever reason, that she should make Cactus remember who he really was. So she recruited Cactus's wife, Colette, and his son, Dewey. In a very sad touch of irony, WCW felt that Cactus's real-life wife was too attractive, so they hired a rather frumpy woman to play her instead.

"Colette" made a plea to Jack, which infuriated his new girlfriend, known as "Bang Bang" (which was formerly Jack's catchphrase). Jack, though, attempting to keep the peace, told his new lover, "Now now, Bang Bang . . . keep an even keel. Don't go raising your colors just because you don't like the cut of her jib." This led to "Colette" running away in tears, with "Dewey" in tow.

So what happened? What was the exciting conclusion, you ask? Well, Cactus made a surprise return at a *Clash of the Champions* special and attacked Vader. You see, this whole thing was just a big setup all along, and Cactus only pretended that he had amnesia in order to get inside Vader's head.

And I am sure that each day, Mick Foley wishes that he really did have amnesia, so that he would never have to remember this putrid angle again.

As 1993 drew to a close, WCW took solace in the fact that while the year had been horrible thus far, they had at least had the foresight to plan *Starrcade* well in advance, with a marquee match that would guarantee a huge buy rate. Vader would be defending the WCW World Title against his former partner, Sid Vicious. After years of being touted as wrestling's next great superstar, Vicious would at last ascend to the throne. WCW would finally have another great babyface to work beside Sting, one who fans would pay to see compete.

Vicious knew it, too. His head began to swell as it filled with thoughts of the gargantuan paydays that being WCW world champion promised. He began to make comments behind the scenes to veteran grapplers who didn't take kindly to being told that their best days were behind them and that he, and he alone, was the future of the company. It was a recipe for disaster.

Things came to a head during WCW's tour of England in September of 1993. Sid was mouthing off to veteran Arn Anderson after a show, once again reiterating the fact that Anderson was old news. Arn finally had enough, and the two went at it. They were restrained by officials. Later that evening, the fight broke out anew, this time with Sid grabbing a pair of plastic safety scissors and attempting to stab Anderson. Both ended up in the hospital. Deportation followed the next day.

It wasn't the first time Sid had used an unorthodox weapon in a real-life fight. Several years prior, he had run into Brian Pillman at a bar, and the two had words. After getting his ass handed to him by Pillman, whom Vicious outweighed by over 100 pounds, Sid left the bar looking for some type of backup. He headed to the local gas station and grabbed a squeegee. Yes, the little rubber brush thing that you soak in water and then rub on your car windows. Surely, with this apparatus on his side, Sid would have the upper hand (and Pillman would wind up squeaky clean). Unfortunately for Vicious, Pillman had already left the bar.

While Vicious received no punishment for the squeegee affair, the scissors fiasco had made the newspapers in England and was therefore something WCW couldn't let slide. Vicious and Anderson were both suspended, with Vicious eventually being fired. This left WCW once again in a precarious position right before its biggest show of the year. And, as they had done in the past, they turned to Ric Flair.

Flair had returned to the promotion earlier in the year after his stint with the WWF. During his WWF tenure, he had won their version of the world title, thus becoming the first man since his namesake, "Nature Boy" Buddy Rogers, to win both the WWF and WCW versions of the belt. Despite this fact, upon returning to WCW he was treated the same way he had been treated since his departure — as a legend, but one no one in the back wanted in the main-event scene.

He was given a talk show segment, "A Flair for the Gold," as a way for WCW to exploit his name value without him actually stepping into the ring. This also allowed Flair to show up on WCW television while adhering to the noncompete clause he had signed after being granted an early release from his WWF contract. The "Flair for the Gold" segment was the location of one of the most comical of all of WCW's mishaps.

Prior to *Fall Brawl 1993*, Davey Boy Smith and Sting appeared on "Flair for the Gold" to confront the team they would face in the big grudge match on the show. While the heel team may have included the likes of Vicious, Vader, and Harlem Heat, the faces had a plan that would shock them — one that would shock the world! And with that introduction, they unveiled their secret weapon: the Shockmaster.

With a huge explosion (again with the explosions), veteran heavyweight Fred Ottman, whom fans knew from previous WWF incarnations as Tugboat and Typhoon, burst through a wall of the set. One problem: he tripped on his way out.

Yes, he fell right on his face, and his mask, which was nothing more than a *Star Wars* Stormtrooper mask covered in silver glitter, fell to the floor. As he stumbled to his feet, you could almost hear the angle screech to a halt. Behind the scenes, though, Ole Anderson continued undeterred, performing a dialogue through his trusty voice box (the same one used for the Black Scorpion fiasco) that resonated over the loudspeakers in the arena, supposedly coming from the Shockmaster himself. It was all too much to bear. Color commentator Jesse Ventura, broadcasting the event live on WTBS, laughed out loud. He was able to compose himself just long enough to snicker, "What an entrance by the Shockmaster!" before losing it again.

Ottman's career never recovered. He spent the remainder of his WCW days as "Uncle Fred," whose gimmick was that he was clumsy. Amazingly, he didn't get over and was shown the door shortly thereafter. Rumors that he tripped on his way out are unsubstantiated.

Another "Flair for the Gold" moment that WCW, and Flair in particular, would surely like to forget was the resurrection of the legendary Four Horsemen. During the late 1980s, the Four Horsemen were Flair's running buddies, a gang of thugs who protected his title at any cost. They had achieved status among fans as a group not to be messed with, and since they were heels, men whom fans desperately wanted to see beaten and bloodied.

The original Horsemen unit consisted of Flair, Tully Blanchard and Arn and Ole Anderson. The plan was made in mid-1993 to reunite the Horsemen in hopes of recapturing the success they had achieved years ago. There was one slight catch, however: while Flair and the Andersons were under contract to WCW, Blanchard was not. Blanchard was offered a paltry amount of money to come back, and he was so insulted that he didn't even return WCW's phone calls. WCW didn't panic, though, as they had a backup plan. They would simply replace Blanchard with Paul Roma.

Who?

Paul Roma. Paul Roma, who was nothing more than a lifetime jobber for the WWF. For no reasons other than he likely worked cheap and had the same hair color as Blanchard, Roma was thrust into a prominent role in the company. Upon his introduction, fans booed. Loudly, and heartily. And it wasn't because the Horsemen were bad guys. This time, they were babyfaces. After nearly six months, Roma turned on Anderson, and this new Horsemen clique was quietly dissolved. Roma bounced around the company for the next year or so before being fired after failing to cooperate in a match with newcomer Alex Wright, who Roma felt was beneath him.

As for Flair, he was finally cleared to compete in the ring and was set for a feud against Rick Rude, who was the reigning WCW International Champion. The International Championship wasn't a real championship at all. The belt was originally the NWA world title. However, WCW decided to leave the NWA and go out on its on, virtually killing the NWA in the process. One slight problem with this situation was that the NWA did, in fact, own the belt that WCW was promoting as a secondary world title, the one Rude was wearing around his waist. Rather than dismiss the belt, WCW decided to continue on with the feud for the championship, but without calling it the NWA title.

Fans didn't care about the so-called championship, but someone within WCW sure did, as Flair and Rude feuded over a big gold belt that was actually called just that — "the big gold belt." After a brief period, someone got the bright idea to create a bogus board of directors called the WCW International Committee and give the title a real name, at which time it became the WCW International Championship.

Fans continued not to care, as they felt there was only one true championship in the promotion, and that was the one around Vader's waist. The same Vader, mind you, who had no opponent for the biggest show of the year following the firing of Sid Vicious.

The same Vader who would now defend the belt against Flair at *Starrcade '93*.

Flair and Vader had an awesome match, with Flair winning the strap. Flair was even given the booking duties, and he proceeded to book several tremendous shows, including *Spring Stampede '94*, in which he defended the title against longtime rival Ricky Steamboat in a classic that tore the house down.

The bean counters, though, did not care about classic matches. They didn't care that the story lines were now coherent, after years of making no sense at all. What they did care about was the bottom line, and despite the fact that Flair had made WCW more enjoyable, fans were not flocking to it the way those in charge felt they should be.

Things had to change. Things were going to change.

Brother.

Hulkster's in the House!

It all changed for WCW in 1994. This was the year that they were no longer the laughingstock of the wrestling business. In fact, this was the year that they were no longer the butt of jokes from the rest of the Turner family. The year of our Lord, nineteen hundred and ninety four, saw the arrival in WCW of the biggest name in the history of pro wrestling and the man who would turn the company around for good.

For 1994 was going to be the year of the Hulkster — even if 1993 had been anything but.

Hogan left the WWF amid a good deal of controversy in the summer of 1993. He had resurfaced after almost a year, at *Wrestlemania IX*, muscling his way into the main-event scene and recapturing the WWF world title. This in and of itself wouldn't have been so unusual, save for the fact that Hogan wasn't even in the main event!

The scheduled main event was to see youthful champion Bret Hart tangle with the 500-pound Yokozuna, a match that Hart was to win. Hogan, however, had other plans. Throwing a hissy fit behind the scenes, Hogan was able to convince Vince McMahon that he, not Hart, should be the world champion. Hart was therefore booked to lose the title, after which Hogan would run down to the ring to "rescue" Hart. Yokozuna issued an immediate challenge to Hogan, who pinned the monster in under a minute, thus making both Bret and Yokozuna look like total losers.

Vince McMahon had a method to his madness. He would allow Hogan to prance around one last time with the belt, provided that Hogan would then lose the belt back to Bret. By beating a legend like Hogan, fans would see that Hart was the champion for a new era, and Hogan could ride off into the sunset with his head held high. Hogan agreed to this before *Wrestlemania*, and, much to the chagrin of the majority of fans, he won the belt. As soon as the belt was in his grasp, Hogan reneged on the promise, and took two months off from defending the belt. McMahon, incensed, had Yokozuna crush Hogan in their rematch to win back the belt. McMahon swore that Hogan would never be seen in the WWF again.

Hogan was fed up as well. He left the ring with no real intention of returning. He opened a restaurant, Pastamania, at the Mall of America in Minnesota, which served such delicacies as Hulkaroos. Despite the sound business strategy of marking up Spaghetti-Os to sell to his loyal fans, the restaurant closed down after just a couple years in business.

With his acting career fading fast, Hogan knew he needed to do something to recapture his mainstream audience. After nearly a year of negotiations, which reportedly involved television and movie possibilities, the immortal Hulk Hogan was about to step back through the ropes, this time with WCW. Hogan made his official entrance into World Championship Wrestling on the June 11, 1994 episode of *WCW Saturday Night*, which was at the time the company's flagship show. A parade was held in Hogan's honor, with all manner of Hulkamaniacs treating him as though Jesus himself was about to put on the tights.

Hogan made his in-ring return on July 17, 1994, at the *Bash at the Beach* pay-per-view, crushing the old guard, Ric Flair, for the WCW championship.

No matter how much Flair meant to the promotion, no matter that Hogan hadn't wrestled a single match for WCW — the past was the past, and it meant nothing. The only thing that mattered to the bookers, to the suits, and to Hogan himself was that the title be placed around his waist immediately.

The initial results were difficult to argue with. The previous pay-per-view, *Slamboree*, had earned an anemic 0.48 buy rate. *Bash at the Beach*, the first pay-per-view of the Hogan era, more than doubled that, topping out at 1.02.

Flair was immediately thrown on the back burner in favor of Hogan. Originally, Flair had been scheduled for one last title reign before dropping the belt again, but Hogan vetoed the idea, his thinking being that he would look weak if he were to lose the belt so soon. Instead of dropping the strap, Hogan was ambushed by a masked man who bashed his knee with a lead pipe. Hogan was shuttled to the hospital, then rushed back to the arena. Barely able to walk, he made his way to the ring. Even without the use of one of his primary limbs, Hogan still held off Flair and kept his belt.

Flair's popularity was definitely becoming a concern to Hogan. Flair was routinely cheered during his feud with Hogan, whom many old-school WCW fans viewed as an unwelcome outsider. Hogan viewed things altogether differently. Here he was, a god among men, and a bunch of rubes preferred to cheer this heel, this villain? This wouldn't work. After all, if he were to enter this penny-ante promotion in an attempt to save it, the last thing he needed was someone who might be able to pull the spotlight away from him. Therefore, it was decided that Flair and Hogan would meet one last time, at *Halloween Havoc*. And this time, it would be in a retirement match.

The match may have been the best of Hogan's career. Flair sold for Hogan as though the very life was being ripped from his being, and he walked Hogan through a masterpiece of a match. It was apparent that the Nature Boy was doing everything he could to cement Hogan as *the* star of WCW, bringing every bit of technical expertise and psychology he had left in his tank.

In return, Hogan brought Mr. T. The tough man who made a living by having a silly haircut and saying, "I pity da fool" was a longtime Hogan crony — the history between the two dated back to the first *Wrestlemania*. Hogan felt that bringing in Mr. T as a special referee would add a bit of spice to the event, which is certainly questionable, since T's real claim to fame, *The A-Team*, hadn't been on the air for almost eight years. Still, as Hogan had learned from Vince McMahon, a celebrity is a celebrity, and it didn't matter what he was famous for or when it happened.

Despite putting up a valiant fight, Flair was once more slain by Hogan's traditional leg-drop finisher. By dropping his "final" match, he paved the way for WCW to become completely rebuilt around Hogan. Immediately following the match, Hogan was attacked again by the mystery man, who was unmasked as longtime Hogan lackey Ed Leslie.

Leslie had garnered a reasonable amount of fame as Brutus Beefcake in the WWF during the late 1980s. He was initially a heel and teamed with veteran grappler Greg Valentine, who carried Beefcake to watchable matches against the tag teams of the day. After a face turn around the time of *Wrestlemania III*, he became Brutus "The Barber" Beefcake, and his gimmick was to render his opponents unconscious and then cut their hair.

As a face with this gimmick, Beefcake was gaining momentum. Of course, it didn't hurt that his best friend behind the scenes was Hogan, who had a great deal of backstage clout. He was on the fast track to success, scheduled to win the promotion's Intercontinental title at the *SummerSlam*

'90 pay-per-view. He would be second behind Hogan himself in the booking plans of the promotion.

Unfortunately for Leslie, tragedy struck. On July 4, 1990, he was parasailing with some friends, working the controls for a boat that was to lift a parasailer into the air. Beefcake turned to face the woman, and her knees slammed into his face. He was rushed to the local hospital and diagnosed with a shattered jaw and nose. His face was completely reconstructed with steel plates and staples in a surgery that lasted nearly nine hours.

Beefcake's WWF career was basically finished at this point. He made a brief appearance the following year as an unnamed wrestler who attacked heels following their matches, but it was dropped shortly thereafter for fear that his face may not be ready for the rigors of a full-time in-ring schedule. Bobby Heenan placed magnets on Beefcake's face (which clung due to the steel within) and ridiculed him on air in an attempt to garner sympathy for the fallen hero. It didn't work, and his last notable WWF match was in a losing effort with Hogan against Money Inc. in a tag match at *Wrestlemania IX*.

When Hogan signed his WCW contract, it gave him immediate pull with the booking committee. It also enabled him to bring his friends along for the ride. And there was no one with whom Hogan was tighter than Ed Leslie.

There was just one slight problem. No one knew the name Ed Leslie. At the time, real names were taboo in the wrestling business, so everyone within used fancy aliases, like Brutus Beefcake. Trouble was, Leslie could no longer use that name; the WWF had it safely under copyright and weren't about to give anyone, especially their largest competitor, any type of advantage. So WCW would need to come up with a different name for Leslie.

At first, he was known as Brother Bruti. Then he was the Clipmaster. But no matter what his name, he always stood by Hogan's side.

After months of following Hogan around like a puppy, Leslie became the evil Butcher, due to the fact that he had "butchered" his friendship with Hogan. The role of the masked man was originally to go to "Mr. Perfect" Curt Hennig, but a deal could not be worked out in time to begin promotion of *Starrcade '94*. With the show fast approaching, Hogan was able to talk the powers that be into giving Leslie the opportunity to headline the biggest show of the year.

You'd think two guys who had been together for years could have a decent match, but you'd be wrong. So very, very wrong. The match, and most of the show, was horrible beyond belief. The event was not only a critical flop, but a financial one as well. The buy rate was 0.6; the previous year's show, which didn't feature Hogan, was a 0.55. While the slight increase may have been considered positive, the fact of the matter was that Hogan's salary alone more than offset the difference.

The booking committee attempted to rectify the situation by dropping Leslie down on the card, and they resurrected the mastodon known as Vader and brought him back as the top contender after months of doing little other than feuding with the Guardian Angel, another Hogan chum. It was somewhat ironic that Vader had been pushed into the background during Hogan's initial WCW tenure; if anyone resembled the type of monster Hogan had faced in feud after feud in the WWF, it was Vader. The 400-pound bonecrusher seemed custom-made for the typical Hogan angle.

The difference was that unlike WWF heels such as King Kong Bundy or John Studd, Vader was *legitimately* tough. If it looked like it hurt, odds are that it really did. He was, after all, the guy who gave Mick Foley concussion after concussion. Hell, he even ripped the poor bastard's ear off!

No wonder Hogan was in no hurry to face him — he knew that Hollywood had never had a leading man who was missing body parts.

Eventually, though, there was no other recourse but to book Hogan vs. Vader. In their very first encounter, Vader unleashed a sneak attack on Hogan, nailing him from behind. He then lifted Hogan high in the air for his patented power bomb, the one that had KO'd Mick Foley, broken the back of a preliminary jobber, and was the E-N-D for anyone unfortunate enough to feel its wrath.

So, of course, Hogan popped right up.

Didn't even sell the move for a second. Didn't act as though it hurt at all. Made not only Vader look like a total wimp, but also everyone else who had ever taken the move and sold it properly. This naturally led fans to foresee the inevitable conclusion of the match: Hogan wins. Vader was understandably infuriated by this but did his best to make Hogan look good throughout their series. Vader eventually turned face, and was scheduled to team with Hogan, but he got into a backstage brawl with Paul Orndorff. He was subsequently fired, then buried on television. He would resurface later in the WWF, but the moment Hogan no-sold the power bomb, Vader's career began a downward spiral from which it would never recover.

Vader wasn't the only one to feel the wrath of Hogan's ego. He was just the one who suffered from it most directly. Some, though, were fortunate that Hogan had come to power in WCW. Many longtime WWF performers who were no longer welcome at McMahon's events were taken in by WCW. Men whom McMahon perceived as no longer having value were now gainfully employed. One such man was John Tenta.

"Hulk was pushing for me," explained Tenta, who was one of Hogan's rivals in the WWF as Earthquake. "First of all, I had to get out of my WWF contract before WCW would even talk to me, and once I did, they were interested. So I went down there and had not too bad of a first year, but it was pretty much downhill after that."

Tenta was a very interesting case. A student of sumo, he came to the WWF and was immediately pushed to the top as Hogan's nemesis. He continued to bounce around the WWF's upper midcard before becoming disenchanted with the scene and returning to Japan. He eventually wound up in WCW under the moniker of Avalanche, due to the fact that the WWF owned the rights to the name Earthquake. He feuded with Sting and other top WCW names before eventually becoming the Shark and joining forces with Kevin Sullivan's band of misfits known as the Dungeon of Doom.

Sullivan didn't look like a wrestler. He was a dwarfish man with a thick Boston accent, who, during his early years in the sport, performed a devil worshipper gimmick, complete with snakes, incantations, and a beautiful valet whom he had turned to the dark side, Fallen Angel. With his days as an in-ring competitor winding down, he had become a member of the booking crew. And he knew that the best way to remain at the top of the card during the twilight of his career was to position himself in a feud with Hulk Hogan.

Kevin had recently turned heel, feuding with his "brother," Dave Sullivan. Except Dave wasn't known as Dave—he was known as Evad. See, he was supposedly dyslexic. And he was really, really stupid. The millions who have dyslexia were no doubt thrilled that they were represented by a character who was a complete moron carrying around a rabbit named Ralph. Then again, this is pro wrestling, a business that has never really concerned itself with good taste.

After splitting from his brainless brother, Kevin went off to form the Dungeon of Doom, a motley collection of thugs obsessed with ending

Hogan's career. During his time as the so-called Taskmaster of the Dungeon of Doom, Sullivan took his orders from his "father," the Wizard. The Wizard was, in actuality, an aging wrestler Sullivan had known for years by the name of Curtis Iaukea, a man whose forehead bore the scars of wars long past—it looked like the Grand Canyon. He bellowed forth his orders to the Dungeon like a carnival barker from hell as he sat atop his throne.

And what a crew he had assembled. Time for a Dungeon of Doom roll call!

Kamala, The Ugandan Headhunter: A cannibal hailing from deepest, darkest Africa, Kamala was a black behemoth who had white stars on each of his sagging boobies and a yellow moon painted on his tummy.

Braun, The Leprechaun: Speaking of yellow moons (and pink hearts, orange stars, blue diamonds, and purple horseshoes), the Dungeon also had their own evil imp. WCW loved their explosions as much as they loved evil imps. Likely inspired by those horrendous *Leprechaun* horror movies, Braun would run around the ring, arms flailing wildly, screaming about his pot of gold.

Meng, The Face of Fear: Meng was a legit tough guy. For some reason, wrestling companies, who promote scripted events where the goal is not to hurt your "opponent," have always had a hard-on for real-life bad asses. Despite lacking charisma and an in-ring style, he was pushed time and again in both the WWF and WCW. As the Face of Fear, he wore a big papier-mâché mask to the ring. It was supposed to resemble an ancient Oriental statue of some sort, but it looked more like a fourth-grader's art project.

Loch Ness: A huge star in England, Giant Haystacks was imported by Sullivan to become the evil Nessie. The result: a handful of the most boring matches fans had ever seen. Loch Ness was so big and immobile that matches couldn't go more than a couple of minutes, tops.

The Zodiac Man: After Ed Leslie took *Starrcade* to new depths, he was turned babyface as the Man with No Name. A week later, he became the Man with No Face. Sadly, he never became the Man with No Job. Instead, he inexplicably turned heel again and became the Zodiac Man. For the part, Leslie had his face painted black and white, as though to symbolize the yin and yang. During interviews, he would simply shout, "Yes! No! Yes! No!" while holding one hand in the air, à la Arnold Horshack.

Things didn't get much better for Leslie. After his run as the Zodiac, he turned face again and became the Booty Man, a gimmick in which he shook his rump. This apparently excited women, who fainted over his fanny. Words on the printed page cannot explain just how wretched this was. The entire persona was focused on Leslie shaking his ass at people while wearing tights with the buttocks cut out. Only a thin, flesh-colored bit of fabric stood between Leslie's bare backside and permanent mental scarring for thousands of wrestling fans. He was given a valet, the Booty Babe, who was, in real life, Kimberly, the gorgeous wife of Diamond Dallas Page. DDP was no doubt delighted that his wife was instructed to act as though she was about to have the Big O as the Booty Man shook his moneymaker in her face. As if things weren't bad enough, his finisher was a high knee to the face. Get it? It was a "heinie!" Only in wrestling could a man get paid to literally make an ass of himself.

The Shark: John Tenta had dropped his Avalanche gimmick to become a man-eater who the Wizard claimed came from "two hundred thousand leagues under the sea." Maybe that was a long-lost sequel to the Jules Verne novel.

Tenta did his best to make the part work. He painted big teeth on his beard and would speak of how he wanted to bite all the little Hulksters.

His greatest sacrifice, however, was the modification of a tattoo on his right bicep. Tenta explains: "I had a tattoo from LSU [Louisiana State University] of a tiger on my arm, and I knew I couldn't be going around with a tiger on my arm, so I got it changed to a shark. Twenty-four hours it took to change this tattoo of a tiger and make it a shark. And, two months later, I wasn't the Shark anymore!"

Got to love the long-term planning of the WCW booking crew.

The Yeti: The Yeti emerged from a huge block of ice during *Halloween Havoc* to become the latest member of Sullivan's circus of the absurd. He was wrapped from head to toe in bandages, as if he'd just come from King Tut's tomb. Why, exactly, a yeti, which has long been depicted as an abominable snowman of some sort, was dressed as a mummy is anyone's guess. What is known is that after his debut, he ran down to the ring and proceeded to grab the Hulkster from behind. He then began to move in a rhythmic manner that looked for all the world like he was dry-humping the poor guy.

Want to talk scary? Someone actually thought that a mummy attempting to invade Hogan's leathery hindquarters would be good for business.

The Giant: At nearly seven feet tall and over 425 pounds, Paul Wight seemed like a "can't miss" prospect. He moved well for a man his size and appeared eager to learn his craft. During his early days in the business, it was not uncommon for him to throw dropkicks, which was unheard of for a guy that large.

WCW decided to try to recapture one of Hogan's greatest rivalries by claiming that Wight was the long-lost son of the legendary Andre the Giant. Some may have found this a wee bit disrespectful; after all, Andre had passed on just a year or so earlier. WCW, though, remained undeterred in their course of action. Even Hogan himself got in on the act, exclaiming at one point, "I'm going to bury you just like I did your father!" The angle was so horrible that it no doubt caused Andre to uncremate himself and then die all over again just so he could be buried and roll over in his grave.

The new Giant and Hogan headlined their first pay-per-view together at *Halloween Havoc '95*. But it wasn't just any match, oh no. It was a sumo monster truck match! Earlier in the year, the Giant had driven a monster truck over the top of one Hogan's prized motorcycles. Hogan was furious and swore revenge. WCW therefore commissioned monster trucks to be built in Hogan and Giant's likenesses. The trucks were then placed on the roof of Detroit's Cobo Hall, and the pair took turns ramming into one another, each hoping to knock this opponent's four-wheeler out of the designated circle.

Hogan won, of course, refusing to lose once again — even in a monster truck match! After "winning," he and the Giant began to fight on the roof of the building. Suddenly, Hulk knocked the big guy off the roof! Everyone was astonished; even Hogan was concerned. The cameras cut back to the arena, where the announce team was in shock. Did the Giant fall to the pavement below? Was he OK? Was he dead? No one knew for sure, but they knew it was bad.

When the scheduled main event of Hogan vs. the Giant for the World Title was to occur, Hogan came to the ring with a worried look on his face. What would he say? Would he apologize to Wight's family? Was the Giant dead? Alive?

He was alive! The Giant came down to the ring for his scheduled match, showing no ill effects. This despite the fact that he had just been thrown off the roof of Cobo Hall. The announce crew was in utter shock. How could this man not only be alive, but also be ready for a wrestling match? They had no explanation. In fact, none was ever given, although Bobby Heenan once claimed that WCW wanted the Giant to come to the ring with a fish in his tights to indicate that he had fallen into the river below.

It's not as though idiotic characters were confined to the Dungeon of Doom, nor were pitiful attempts to re-create past WWF successes the domain of the Giant alone. Prior to *Uncensored '95*, Hogan began blabbermouthing about an "ultimate" surprise that he was going to unveil at the pay-per-view. By even saying the "u" word, Hogan knew that the fans would be expecting the Ultimate Warrior to be the next to join the cavalcade of WWF rejects. Despite the fact that WCW wasn't even close to signing the Warrior, Hogan and the WCW booking crew kept up the façade. Not a single broadcast went by without some mention of the "ultimate" surprise.

After months of buildup, fans were certainly expecting WCW to deliver. And deliver they did: the biggest knock-off since Mr. Pibb. Behold The Renegade, who ran down to the ring just like the Ultimate Warrior, shook the ropes just like the Ultimate Warrior, and had face paint just like the Ultimate Warrior. But despite what the shills at WCW would have the fans believe, he was assuredly not the Ultimate Warrior.

He was Rick Williams, an independent wrestler who had made his way to WCW under the guise of Reo, Lord of the Jungle. The WCW booking crew decided that Williams looked enough like Warrior to attempt the experiment, with Hogan championing the idea all the way. Williams, no doubt thinking he would be a fool to pass up this chance for instant notoriety, jumped at the opportunity and began studying tapes of the Warrior's entrance and mannerisms.

WCW immediately pushed Renegade to the moon. Within months of his arrival, Renegade was put over Arn Anderson in a match that Double A has called the worst of his career. Perhaps Williams had studied the Warrior's paper-thin playbook a little too well; Renegade displayed almost no technical ability in the ring whatsoever, which led to matches that uniformly sucked. He teamed with the major names of the period, such as Hogan and Sting. They had him squash jobber after jobber in an effort to make him look like the second coming of the Warrior. In the end, though, the fans just weren't buying what Williams was selling.

He dropped the TV belt to Dallas Page at *Fall Brawl*, after which manager Jimmy Hart turned on him. Hart wiped the makeup from Renegade's face, exclaiming, "You're not the Renegade! You're just Rick! You're nothing!" Instead of hating Hart for his comments, fans pretty much agreed. This so-called Renegade really wasn't anything more than a fraud from the get-go. He fell off the map, returning only sporadically to TV, most notably as the "fake" Ultimate Warrior in an angle at *Fall Brawl '98*.

In late 1998, Williams's contract expired and WCW chose not to renew it. The WWF had little to no interest in him either, and Williams fell into a deep despair. This eventually led him to put a gun to his head and end his own life on February 23, 1999. He was only 33 years old.

A sad story, made even more depressing due to the fact that others who had suffered through bad gimmicks early in their WCW careers were actually able to rebound from the experience. With the influx of Hogan flunkies, many people who had slaved for WCW during its dark period of the early '90s were treated like rubbish. Men such as Steve Austin and Mick Foley departed the promotion in hopes of finding opportunities elsewhere, preferably somewhere far away from Hogan's shadow.

Hogan's ego was driving not just wrestlers away from the promotion, but fans as well. And nowhere was this more evident that at *Uncensored '96*. WCW's goal with *Uncensored* was to promote it as the wildest event of their year. Most matches were conducted under some type of gimmick, be it no DQ, cage, or some other bizarre stipulation. At the inaugural event, Dustin Rhodes and the Black Top Bully wrestled on the back of a moving 18-wheeler, with the goal being to honk a horn. With a pedigree such as this, was there ever a doubt the show would make it to a second year?

The main event of the 1996 version was a Doomsday match in a triple-decker cage where Hogan and Randy Savage took on eight men. Yes, two versus eight; but remember, one of those two was Hulk Hogan. The opening segment of the match saw Savage and Hogan obliterate Flair, who had returned from retirement to sustain even more beatings from Hogan, enabling the dynamic duo to descend into the second cage. There they brutalized Lex Luger, Kevin Sullivan, Barbarian, and Meng. Hogan locked the rule breakers in another part of the cage.

This two-on-eight match was becoming a massacre — with the two demolishing the eight! The tide turned, however, when Jeep Swenson, who would go on to star as Bane in the horrific *Batman & Robin*, came down and attacked Hogan. Shocking that Hogan sold for none of the wrestlers, but did for an actor. A pathetic and insulting aside about Swenson's character: in the days leading up to the match, he was known as the Final Solution. Apparently, someone from the Jewish faith must have clued them in that maybe, just *maybe*, that wasn't the greatest ring name in the world, since it also referred to Hitler's plan to exterminate the Jews. So he was re-renamed the Ultimate Solution, which, of course, didn't change the fact that the guy still stunk up the ring.

And then, as if this match wasn't painful enough, out came Zeus, Hogan's old nemesis from *No Holds Barred*! It was something no sane fan ever wanted to see again. Bringing him in was yet another instance of WCW officials kowtowing to Hogan's whims.

The Doomsday match ended, of course, with Savage and Hogan coming out on top. And, naturally, it was Ric Flair who took the fall. WCW announcers claimed the match was bigger than the World Series and the Super Bowl combined, but obviously viewers didn't agree, as the show drew almost a third fewer buys than the previous year's *Uncensored* had.

Finally, even WCW officials could no longer handle Hogan's ego. More importantly, those in charge were starting to have a tough time justifying Hogan's huge contract. Not only were buy rates sliding, but ratings were in the crapper as well.

Eric Bischoff, though, hadn't come this far to fail due to one man's ego —unless that ego was his own. He was the man who had taken control of WCW and pleaded with Turner to open the checkbook and import Hogan and his other WWF friends. By doing this, Bischoff had brought a level of legitimacy to the promotion. In fact, he had also convinced Turner to open up a slot on prime-time television with the creation of *Nitro*, which went head-to-head every Monday night with the WWF's *Raw*. If anyone had ever had a chance at beating the WWF, it was Bischoff, and nothing was going to stop him now.

See, Bischoff had an idea. One that would make WCW's *Nitro* not just the number one pro wrestling show, but the number-one show in all of cable television. One that would give Hulk Hogan one last ride to the top of the mountain. One that would bring WCW to greater heights than it had ever reached before.

The nWo invasion was about to begin.

And even the almighty Vince McMahon had no idea just how far-reaching its impact would be.

But, ironically, neither did Eric Bischoff.

Moonlighting

When Hulk Hogan had left the WWF for WCW, Vince McMahon didn't sweat it. Vince didn't sweat much of anything. As he watched Hogan's early days in WCW, he knew that he had made the correct decision in showing Hogan the door. He was right, as usual. Hogan's ego was out of control, and now, finally, someone else had to put up with it. Let them have the fun of shuffling main events to Hogan's liking, McMahon thought. Hogan was old, way past his prime. Everyone knew it, except those jokers down in Atlanta.

McMahon didn't need Hulk Hogan. Anyone could be Hulk Hogan with McMahon's marketing genius behind them. In fact, he would make a new Hulk Hogan. A younger Hulk Hogan, one who was more athletic, with a better body, one who would obey his commands without question. He just needed someone strong and handsome, a guy with a wholesome, all-American attitude.

He had that in Lex Luger. Luger had made a name for himself in the old NWA region, going on to become WCW World Champion in 1991. It was something fans had been expecting Luger to do for a loooong time, as he had been viewed as a future world champion since his debut in the business in the mid-1980s. He had been in many programs in which he chased the world title but inevitably came up short. Fans labeled him a "choke" artist.

He was the first champion for WCW following the departure of Ric Flair, a none-too-envious position. For while fans hated Flair the character, they loved Flair the wrestler. If ever the term "love to hate" applied to a wrestler, it applied to Ric Flair. Fans paid to see Flair get his licks. When Flair left the promotion, it was as though the heart was ripped out of the fans. Luger's title reign will best be remembered not for any specific match or event, but rather for the resonant chants of "We want Flair!" in every arena in which he appeared.

Luger left WCW, and, like many others, decided that he no longer wanted anything to do with wrestling. When he signed with Vince McMahon, many felt that he had been lying through his teeth about retirement. He hadn't. He had no intention of stepping through the ropes again. He hadn't signed with the World Wrestling Federation; he had signed to be the spokesperson for McMahon's fledgling World Bodybuilding Federation.

The WBF was the first of McMahon's many attempts to diversify his business. Being a huge fan of bodybuilding, he decided to create an organization that would promote muscle contests and sell a supplement called ICOPRO. With Luger, he could draw in those WWF fans who weren't familiar with bodybuilding. He realized that he needed to make an impact within the bodybuilding industry, however, and he chose to do so at the Mr. Olympia competition, the largest contest of the year.

During the weekend's festivities, McMahon rented a small booth, under the pretense that he was looking to start up a fitness magazine, one with a bit more pizzazz than the dry muscle periodicals of the day. Of course, anyone who knew McMahon should have known he wasn't there simply to shill a magazine.

At the conclusion of the Mr. Olympia contest, Tom Platz, one of McMahon's new employees, took the stage. No one suspected anything, as Platz was a well-respected member of the bodybuilding community. They may not have suspected Platz, but they should have suspected his boss. When Platz began to speak, he shocked everyone by announcing the formation of the World Bodybuilding Federation, which would, in his words, "kick Mr. Olympia's ass!" McMahon then attempted, in a single night, to sign all of Mr. Olympia's top stars right out from under the old promotion's nose.

Sound familiar?

Indeed, McMahon used the same tactics that had brought him success in the wrestling community. He threw money around like it was going out of style. He flew potential employees first class to Stamford, Connecticut, home of the WWF headquarters, put them up in five-star hotels, and did everything he could to make them feel as though this were an opportunity they couldn't pass up.

The biggest lure, of course, was the money. Gary Strydom, whom McMahon viewed as a can't-miss prospect, was given almost half a million dollars per year. Even those on the lower end of the WBF spectrum made around a quarter million a year. It was an insane amount of money. No one within the industry had ever made that kind of jack before.

It wasn't just well-known bodybuilders of the day he was after, though. He wanted to sign anyone remotely identified with the sport. Lou Ferrigno, best known for his stint on the TV show *The Incredible Hulk*, in which he played the title character, was brought into the promotion. With the stars of his new business signed, McMahon got the go-ahead from the USA Network, the home to the WWF at the time, for a weekly show. *WBF Bodystars* aired on Saturday mornings and was hosted by Luger, who promised to strengthen couch potatoes sitting at home "fourteen different ways."

The show's primary purpose, of course, was to hype the inaugural WBF pay-per-view, which took place at the Trump Taj Mahal in Atlantic City on June 15, 1991. McMahon spared no expense for the show, constructing an elaborate stage and using smoke machines and a complex lighting scheme. In a stroke of genius, McMahon even brought in Regis Philbin to host the event. Because, when you think of muscle heads posing in G-strings that barely cover their shrunken genitals, you think Regis Philbin.

McMahon hoped to bring the flash of the WWF to bodybuilding and create an entirely new sport. Personas were created for each of the body-builders. There was the Dark Angel, performing a *Phantom of the Opera* gimmick, and the Executioner, complete with guillotine. The highlight, though, was the Flexing Dutchman, whom the commentators fawned over, stating, "Well, you've heard of a Dutch oven? This Dutchman has them heated up." For those who don't know about such things—and be thankful you don't—"Dutch oven" is a slang term for farting in bed and holding your partner's head under the covers.

Which is a pretty good description of the event. The show was a complete and utter disaster, with a laughable buy rate. Looking back, it shouldn't have come as a shock. The old-school bodybuilding fans scoffed at the silly outfits and personas. Wrestling fans stayed away because, despite the out-landish costumes, it wasn't wrestling. McMahon took a bath on the entire promotion, eventually losing some $15 million and getting stuck with a huge stockpile of ICOPRO in the process.

It probably wouldn't have mattered if the league had been successful. In late 1993, McMahon was indicted on steroid charges, which immediately put a black cloud over everything he did. A bodybuilding federation of muscle-bound freaks was the last thing he needed to be associated with. Though he was eventually acquitted, the effect on the performers in the

WWF was noticeable. Hugely muscled men such as Hogan, Warlord, and others all disappeared from the company.

One notable musclehead remained, though: Lex Luger. McMahon still had Luger under contract from the WBF days, so it seemed foolish not to use him. The WWF convinced Luger to get back into the ring, teaming him with Bobby Heenan and adopting the character of the Narcissist. As the Narcissist, Luger would stare into the mirror, commenting on how fabulous he looked. This was probably not far removed from what happened in his house on a daily basis.

The Narcissist lasted less than six months, as Hulk Hogan's departure from the company opened up the number-one babyface spot on the roster. With a quick change in philosophy, Luger abandoned the Narcissist gimmick and wrapped himself in the American flag, becoming "Made in the U.S.A." Lex Luger. He immediately went after the WWF world champ, a 500-pound Samoan named Yokozuna who had pledged his allegiance to Japan. Vince McMahon dubbed Luger part of the "new generation," the idea being that Hogan and his lackeys were yesterday's news.

As a way of gathering support for Luger's main-event run, the WWF commissioned the building of a bus. Yes, a bus, like what kids ride to school. But this wasn't just any old bus—it was the Lex Express! Luger traveled across the country promoting, well, himself. He would stop at various locations and pose with kids at hospitals. He would sign autographs. He would smile and kiss babies. Footage was shown each week of Luger riding in the bus, sleeping in the bus, looking out the window of the bus—all of which made for thrilling TV.

After months of touring the country in the Lex Express, Luger finally arrived at *SummerSlam* for his showdown with Yokozuna. Yokozuna's manager came up with a stipulation that this would be Luger's first and only title shot. With everything on the line, Luger beat the big guy in the match, and all the good guys lifted Luger on their shoulders as red, white, and blue balloons fell from the ceiling.

The only problem was that Luger had won the match by count-out. According to the rules of pro wrestling, this means that the champion keeps his belt. Luger hadn't really won at all. He had choked once again.

The plan originally was to have Luger win the belt at *Wrestlemania X*, some nine months later. In the meantime, he would feud with Ludvig Borga, a Finnish badass who had no love for the U.S.A. Borga hated the U.S. for a unique reason: he was an environmentalist. During his introductory vignettes, he would walk along streams, noting the horrific pollution in this country. Then he would state that in Finland, the land was without filth. This would somehow cause the fans to hate him. One could almost imagine him growling, "Give a hoot, don't pollute!" like Woodsy the Owl with an evil foreign accent.

Borga wasn't the only guy with a persona that didn't click. Remember poor Mike Shaw, the guy WCW dressed up as an escapee from a mental institution, and then inexplicably converted to a truck driver? Believe it or not, the WWF came up with not just one bad gimmick for Shaw, but two. His first gimmick was that of holy man Friar Ferguson. He came down the aisle to the sound of Gregorian chants, splashing holy water on the fans. Maybe the promotion was planning on running shows at monasteries.

It wasn't the first time wrestling fans had called for a separation of church and ring. In the late 1980s, the WWF had created a bogus southern preacher by the name of Brother Love. "I love yeeeewwwww," he'd whine, as fans booed mercilessly. At least in this case it was justified, as the phony pastor was actually cast as a heel, a play on televangelists of the time, such as Jerry Falwell.

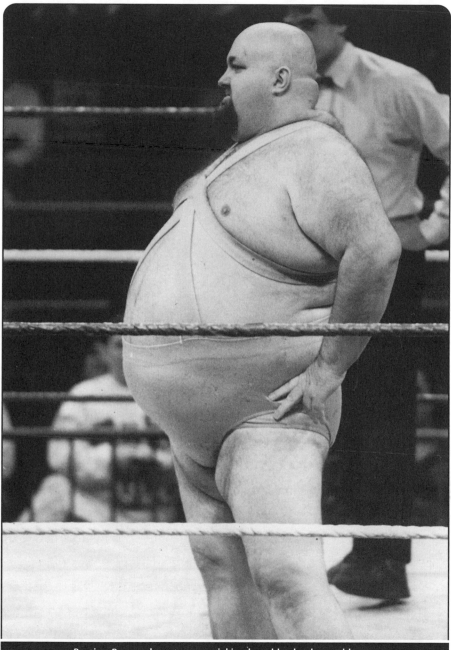

Bastion Booger, hero to nose-picking hunchbacks the world over.

Friar Ferguson, however, wasn't a witty commentary on American society. It was just a dumb gimmick that no one liked. The WWF realized this and came up with an idea a million times worse. Looking at Shaw's rather fleshy physique, the creative team wondered if fans might boo someone simply because he was disgusting to look at. Thus, Bastion Booger was born.

Shaw's bulbous, hairy body was shoehorned into a dingy gray outfit with strips of cloth covering his upper torso. The rear of the costume was fashioned in such a manner that the top of his back was squished into a hump. (What is it with wrestling promoters and hunchbacks?) Sometimes he'd pick his nose. Other times, he'd be more sophisticated and simply eat food out of a garbage can. His entrance "music" was nothing more than the sounds of burps and flatulence.

Think about that. Someone actually thought this would encourage fans to buy tickets. Not only did someone get paid to portray a fat guy picking his nose, but also someone else got paid to think up the idea. And someone else, someone high up in the company, approved the idea.

It was by no means the only horrible idea the WWF came up with during this period. How about Max Moon? He was a spaceman from Uranus. Well, maybe not, but he definitely came from someone's anus. Moon was scheduled for big things in the WWF. He was originally portrayed by Mexican wrestling legend Konnan, but a falling out backstage caused the gimmick to be handed off to lifetime jobber Paul Diamond. Why did Diamond get this gig? Because the suit fit, silly. It was a far-out costume that had weird rings around its arms, making Diamond look as though he was ribbed, like one of those condoms "made for her pleasure." The kicker was the jetpack on the back of the suit that was to lift the spaceman into the ring. Sadly, the gizmo never quite worked out, so Max had to jump up the ring steps while small puffs of smoke emanated from his backside.

There was also Men on a Mission, a tag team from the hood led by rapping manager Oscar. "Here comes Oscar, Mabel, and Mo! Everybody say yo yo yo!" It was just like WCW's P.N. News, except now there were three hefty fools assaulting fans' eardrums and eyeballs. After a couple of years, the team split up, and the larger member of the duo, a 500-pounder by

JOHN LAWSON

Oh my *God*, that poor rope! Men on a Mission's Mabel shows you his better side.

the name of Mabel, was given a push for no reason other than he was big and fat. This led to some of the worst main events, both financially and critically, in WWF history.

It wasn't just midcarders who were stuck with such miserable personas. Former main-eventers were given new identities as well. Ricky Steamboat had made a name for himself back at *Wrestlemania III*, winning the Intercontinental belt from "Macho Man" Randy Savage in a five-star classic that's still talked about today. He followed that performance up by jumping to WCW and feuding with Ric Flair in unquestionably the greatest feud of all time.

Just one problem with Steamboat: Vince McMahon didn't like him.

McMahon and Steamboat had issues going back to the days following Steamboat's win over Savage. Steamboat's wife had just given birth to their first son. Steamboat requested a couple of weeks off. McMahon felt this was completely out of line and had Steamboat drop his strap to the Honky Tonk Man, who at the time was still a joke wrestler. After the Flair series, though, McMahon felt that bringing Steamboat back was in his best interest. He didn't want to promote the guy, but rather to have him under contract just so WCW couldn't use him to their advantage.

Steamboat had long used the moniker of "The Dragon," and the creative department liked that a lot. So much so, in fact, that they wanted him to become a real-life, fire-breathing dragon. An outfit was fashioned with scales, fins, and a giant tail. Steamboat would walk to the ring with a torch and a mouthful of gasoline. As the lights dimmed, he would spray the gas onto the torch, creating a giant fireball that lit up the darkened arena.

McMahon instructed his announcers to act as though Steamboat was a newcomer to the world of wrestling. He was not to be referred to as "Ricky Steamboat," but simply as "The Dragon." Steamboat put up with this for about a year before heading back to WCW, once again putting on amazing bouts with Flair.

Steamboat was just one legend the WWF felt the need to embarrass. For years, the tag team known as the Road Warriors was the most feared combination in the business. They ran roughshod over any opponent in their path, drawing huge crowds with their wild face paint and brutal style. Vince brought them in during the early 1990s to feud with Demolition, a tandem the WWF had created as Road Warrior clones.

After the Warriors wiped out Demolition, the promotion had little idea what to do with them. Hawk and Animal disappeared from WWF television for several months, finally reappearing with Paul Ellering, who had managed the pair during their NWA days. While this would likely have been the spark the duo had been missing, the WWF felt they needed something else.

Something like a ventriloquist's dummy.

Yes, the Monsters of the Midway, the infamous Legion of Doom, were led to the ring by a ventriloquist's dummy named Rocco. Hawk and Animal were pushed into the background, and Rocco became the star of the show. It didn't take long for the Warriors to get sick of that, and they too left not only the promotion, but the entire business as well!

Others stuck around no matter what they were given to work with. The Undertaker, for example, had become one of the Federation's most popular characters. That didn't excuse him from being part of one of the most idiotic angles of all time. During early 1994, Taker was scheduled to take a few months vacation from the road, as he had been going nonstop since his arrival in 1990. Instead of having a heel administer a beatdown that would explain his absence, the promotion booked him into a no-DQ casket match at the *Royal Rumble* against then-champion Yokozuna.

With the help of every rule breaker from the locker room, the Japanese behemoth was able to steal Undertaker's urn from his manager, Paul Bearer. Remembering that Undertaker derived his power from the urn, Yoko cracked it open. Green smoke began to billow from the vessel, and Undertaker slowly withered to the mat. Yokozuna was then able to throw the undead zombie into the casket and claim victory, thus reaffirming that old adage, "Fat Samoans who pledge their allegiance to Japan and steal mystical urns are tough to beat."

As the bad guys wheeled Undertaker's coffin to the back, it began to spew forth a green smoke not unlike that which had come from the urn. Suddenly, the lights went out, and a bell tolled. A vision appeared on the video wall: the Undertaker, presumably inside the casket. Good thing Vince had invested in that "casketcam" before the match!

The Undertaker then recited a most bizarre monologue: "Be not proud, for the soul of the Undertaker lives within the spirit of all mankind, the eternal flame of life that cannot be extinguished, the origin of which cannot be explained. The answer lies in the everlasting spirit. Soon, all mankind will witness the rebirth of the Undertaker. I will not rest in peace."

Lightning and more smoke followed, as an x-ray of the Undertaker ascended toward the ceiling on the video screens. As the image left the screen, a shadowy figure floated upward to heaven.

Uh huh.

At least Mark Calloway (the man who portrayed the Undertaker) finally had a few months off the road. He'd need the rest, because the WWF had another craptastic story line dreamed up for his return. Occasionally during his absence, the company would air footage of regular citizens speaking of Undertaker sightings. You know, like an Elvis sighting, but with an undead zombie wrestler in place of the King of Rock and Roll.

After a few months of this, evil millionaire Ted DiBiase appeared on WWF TV stating that he would be bringing the Undertaker back. Paul Bearer, Undertaker's longtime manager, vehemently denied DiBiase's claims. In order to clear up the confusion, the WWF brought in Leslie Nielsen, best known for his role as Lt. Frank Drebin in the *Naked Gun* films. His goal of finding the Undertaker was played out over several weeks in a series of skits that were as funny as repeated blows to the nuts with a blunt object.

Finally, DiBiase did just what he promised, delivering the Undertaker to WWF audiences. Bearer cried foul, claiming DiBiase's Undertaker was a fraud. The two managers decided to have their respective charges meet at the upcoming *SummerSlam* pay-per-view. During the match, three things became immediately apparent:

1. Bearer's Undertaker was at least four or five inches taller than DiBiase's.
2. DiBiase's Undertaker's face didn't look anything like Bearer's.
3. Fans really hated this whole angle.

The WWF had been planning for an extended series of Undertaker vs. Underfaker matches, but the reaction of the live crowds was so negative that they killed off the character immediately following their first encounter.

Brian Lee, a real-life friend of Mark Calloway, played the Underfaker. In order to get Lee ready for the role, a prelim jobber named Pete Polaco (who worked as P.J. Walker) took bumps while Calloway looked on, ensuring that Lee had his mannerisms down. As a way of "repaying" Polaco for his work behind the scenes, the WWF outfitted him with a new identity as well. He would become Aldo Montoya, Portuguese Man of War.

Now you're probably thinking that naming a wrestler after a jelly-fish, no matter how lethal it may be, is a bad idea. And you're right. What's worse is that for some completely unknown reason, the WWF outfitted Aldo with a yellow mask that for all the world looked like a jockstrap. Fans laughed as Montoya's ridiculous outfit, which is a shame, as Montoya was actually one of the better workers in the company at the time.

Truthfully, the abilities of a wrestler didn't seem to matter, because at this point, the WWF creative department was once again simply throwing things against the wall to see what would stick. It seemed as if they would look out the windows of Titan Towers to come up with the persona of the week. Every wrestler on the roster seemed to have another career that more clearly defined his persona than anything he did in the ring.

T.L. Hopper, for instance, was the wrestling plumber. He would venture to the ring to the sound of toilets flushing, bedecked in a dirty shirt, with conspicuous brown marks on his pants. And, yes, his butt crack would be showing. He wouldn't be much of a stereotypical plumber without that! He would carry Betsy, his filthy plunger, to the ring, and he'd shove her in his defeated opponent's face. For, you see, he wasn't just a wrestling plumber, he was an *evil* wrestling plumber.

Or how about Duke "The Dumpster" Droese? He was a garbageman. Know how we knew that? Because he would carry a garbage can to the ring. He was billed as being from Mount Trashmore, which certainly sounds like a lovely place to raise a family. When he won, he would dump the contents of his trash can onto his opponent. This was somehow supposed to make him a fan favorite.

Back on the evil side of things was the nefarious Repo Man. Vignettes aired in which he would repossess items that folks were late in paying. Even if you were just an hour late on your payment, he might repossess your house. One time, he was tracking down a guy who was late on his car payment, and he spotted the deadbeat's kid. Since he couldn't find the dad, he stole the kid's bike as a way of payment. He wore a silly little Lone Ranger-style mask to hide his identity, along with a trenchcoat with "Repo Man" spelled out in license plates. He had pieces of old car tires on his shoulders. He'd sneak everywhere he went, even to the ring as his entrance was announced over the public address system.

Repo Man was actually Barry Darsow, who had won the WWF tag belts three times as half of Demolition. After the Road Warriors destroyed Demolition, there wasn't much left for him to do. Darsow was unique in that he played the horrible Repo Man character so far over the top that it was hard to hate the guy, despite WWF's hopes that the deadbeats in the audience would boo him. With conflicting fan sentiment, he never really got over, and he left the WWF with a whimper.

Tito Santana was a huge star for the WWF in the mid-1980s, often wearing the Intercontinental or Tag Team belts. In the early 1990s, however, the promotion felt that Tito was a bit long in the tooth, and they altered his identity. Grabbing his copy of *Insulting Stereotypes for Dummies*, McMahon came up with the idea of El Matador, the world's first pro wrestling bullfighter.

Santana was shown on WWF television fighting an actual, live bull. Of course, unless they wanted Tito to be gored, safety precautions had to be taken. The video crew used one of the oldest tricks in the book. They filmed Tito up close then showed stock footage of a bullfight from what appeared to be the roof of the arena. It looked like an Ed Wood movie. Somehow, this was supposed to help him in the ring, because bullfighting and wrestling are so similar. *¿Qué?*

At least the WWF finally had a worthy opponent lined up for him: Mantaur. Half-man, half-beast, all crap. Imagine a guy dressed up as a bull, complete with pelt and the real-life head of an ox. The headgear was actually so tall that the poor guy had to look out through the mouth hole to see where he was going. It was as if a taxidermist were put in charge of creating costumes for Disney World.

Sadly, Mantaur didn't wrestle with the gear on. He would remove it and then begin to shamble about the ring like a bull, shuffling his hooves and charging his opponent. As if all that weren't menacing enough, he would also moo. Yes, just like a cow.

Only slightly less bizarre was Phantasio, the wrestling magician. Wearing a top hat and carrying a cane, he was only a monocle away from becoming wrestling's answer to Mr. Peanut. After a prematch shenanigan or two, the magic would begin. That is, if you replace the word "magic" in the previous sentence with your favorite synonym for feces.

For his greatest feat of magic, Phantasio would reach into the back of his opponent's tights and pull off his rival's underwear. The rival, rightfully stunned, would then be prey to a schoolboy roll-up and pin. Ladies and gentlemen, the worst finisher of all time: the Magic Wedgie.

Sound painful? Sure! But so is a trip to the dentist. There's an idea! How about an evil dentist? His name was Dr. Isaac Yankem, DDS. Get it? I Yankem! And he had bad teeth. He was a dentist with bad teeth. See the irony? Wouldn't you want to plunk down your hard-earned money to see a wrestling dentist with bad teeth?

No? Well, maybe you'd rather see a comedy act. How about Who? Who?

Who, that's who. A masked wrestler based on the 40-year-old Abbott and Costello routine "Who's on First?" This bit was based on the premise of two guys discussing a baseball game in which the first baseman is named "Who" and the second baseman is named "What." When the straight man asks, "Who's on first?" the other guy says, "Right. And What's on second." The straight guy then comes back with, "But who's on first?"

Isn't that funny? Someone in the Federation certainly thought so, because they threw Jim Neidhart under a mask as Who. Entire matches would be commentated using the schtick, and damn did it get old fast.

Then there was Battle Kat, who wore a cat costume and mask and moved around the ring like a feline. His finisher was the Kat's Kradle, which unfortunately didn't entail making elaborate shapes out of string until his opponent fell asleep. That wouldn't have made much sense, but then a wrestler dressed up like Hello Kitty doesn't make a lot of sense, either.

Nor did Bertha Faye, white trash woman wrestler. Importing Rhonda Singh, who had gained a reputation as a brute on the Japanese women's wrestling scene as Monster Ripper, was a solid move by the company. Outfitting her in garish costumes and skintight fishnets over her massive thighs wasn't. Nor was forbidding her to use any of the power moves that had garnered her fame in Japan. But there she was, spayed of anything that made her valuable in the ring, because that wouldn't fit the character. Instead, she skipped around the ring with her pigtails like a little girl, WWF officials hoping that fans would boo her simply because she was such an eyesore.

The company also decided that it would be a good idea to mock other sports, so they created a whole line of bogus sports wrestlers. Words cannot describe the stupidity of this idea, as most wrestling fans are also fans of real sports. There was Thurman "Sparky" Plugg, who was a good ol' boy race car driver; the Goon, a hockey player so rough that he was supposedly thrown out of the NHL; and, of course, Abe "Knuckleball" Schwartz, aka MVP: Most Violent Player. The latter was the WWF's attempt to capitalize on Major League Baseball's 1994 players' strike. The promotion was trying to say that while those other, so-called "legitimate" sports were just out to steal money from the audience, the WWF was there solely for the fans. Spots were aired stating that the WWF would never go on strike. Of course they wouldn't — Vince McMahon would never allow his boys to form a union!

Abe Schwartz was created to be the face and voice of these commercials. Here was an evil baseball player hailing from Cooperstown, home of the Baseball Hall of Fame, yelling at the fans and doing anything he wanted. His entrance music was "Take Me Out to the Ballgame," which sounded as if it were being performed by the Jake Roberts Moonshine Jug Band. Just in case someone in the audience still didn't understand the character, he would carry a big sign that read, "I'm on strike." Vince McMahon is right up there with Ian ("Pussy Galore") Fleming in the creation of subtle characters.

Characters like Xanta Klaus. He was the evil brother of Santa Claus. He lived at the South Pole, not the North Pole, and he went down the chimney to steal presents from good little girls and boys. He was covered in black with red trim, and he shouted "Ho, ho, ho!" in a manner most vile. Before this could go too far, however, someone in creative actually looked at a calendar and, realizing that Christmas only comes once every twelve months, scrapped the idea because the character would only be viable for a short period each year.

Unfortunately, other similarly grand visions weren't nixed. Before you read another word, please stop and look at the top right corner of the front cover of the book in your hands. Do you see that Bigfoot-looking creature? His name was Giant Gonzalez, and the WWF had *huge* plans for him. They had big plans for a guy in a bodysuit that was painted with muscles (including a butt crack) and covered with fur. Plans for a man who was possibly the worst wrestler in history.

"But wait," you're no doubt saying. "Earlier in the book, that title was awarded to WCW's El Gigante."

Same guy.

For no reason other than the fact that he was really, really tall, the WWF floated a contract to Jorge Gonzalez after his disastrous run in WCW.

Thinking he would be an excellent opponent for the Undertaker, they had the two engage in a series of matches that redefined the term *atrocious*.

Which would also describe the most infamous of all the mid-1990s WWF gimmicks, Doink the Clown. Yes, a wrestling clown, complete with greasepaint and bright-green wig.

One wrestling clown was bad enough...

Sounds like a dumb idea, and it was. But as unbelievable as it may seem, Doink was originally a brilliantly cast figure, with veteran Matt Borne playing the role to perfection. You see, he wasn't a friendly clown, but rather an evil clown who played dirty tricks on his opponents. He'd come out to happy circus music that would quickly change to a haunting melody, complete with cackles and screams. He'd pop little kids' balloons with a lit cigar. One time, he hit his opponent with a car battery.

The character was so well done that Doink was beginning to get over with the fans. Since the gimmick was gaining in popularity, a second Doink

(Steve Keirn, last seen as Skinner, the alligator man) was added in an attempt to create more mayhem. Instead, it watered down the gimmick. What really killed it dead, however, was the fact that Borne was facing "personal demons," and you know what that means. Borne was let go from the company, and various wrestlers took over the part of the clown.

Even with Borne gone, Vince decided to push the character, turning him face, which took away any coolness factor that a wrestling clown may have. Hard to explain why an evil clown is good in wrestling but a nice clown

...but then the idea really got out of hand.

isn't, but that's the case. Things got substantially worse for Doink when a midget sidekick, Dink, was added. Later, a whole litter of midget clowns was added, including Pink and Wink. Fans completely turned on the character, with chants of "Kill the clown!" becoming commonplace at WWF events.

And that was really the problem: the WWF simply could not figure out what the fans wanted to see. Nearly every act made fans wonder just what the hell they were watching. Business was in the toilet, and it appeared as though it was only a matter of time before the company went completely broke.

To make matters worse, WCW's *Nitro* had just shown up on Turner Network Television, giving fans an alternative to the WWF. When the industry heard about this, everyone save Eric Bischoff thought it was a horrible idea, and that WCW would once again be a laughingstock.

They couldn't have been more wrong. On September 4, 1995, WCW launched *Nitro*, featuring Sting vs. Ric Flair, a fantastic, high-flying match of Brian Pillman and Japanese sensation Jushin Liger, and the shocking WCW return of Lex Luger—shocking because the WWF was advertising him for upcoming shows, believing they had him under contract. They didn't. His contract had expired, and Vince had forgotten to renew it.

Bischoff, who, in addition to being the mastermind behind WCW was also its lead announcer, had other tricks up his sleeve as well. He would find out the match results on *Raw* (not hard to do, since the WWF taped weeks in advance) and announce them on *Nitro*, which was live every week. He had a monitor at his broadcast position that showed what *Raw* was doing so he could counterprogram on the fly. He booked shocking events that made fans afraid not to watch for fear that they might miss something big.

His work paid off. Bischoff's *Nitro* beat *Raw* in the ratings the very first night. For the next year or so, it was a dead heat between the two shows, something no one save Bischoff even dreamed was possible. WCW was really breathing down the WWF's neck, and in the eyes of many, it was now the new number-one wrestling promotion in the country.

McMahon was embarrassed and angry. Turner's rasslin' company was tied with the WWF for number one. How? How the hell could these hicks from Atlanta be putting up such a fight?

It wasn't his fault. It couldn't be. He was Vincent Kennedy McMahon, damn it! It wasn't his fault.

It was the government's fault. Yes! That's it, that's it exactly. It was the fucking government's fault, for making him defend himself against the steroid accusations. That's what it was. Had to be. He had to worry about staying out of the slammer, and due to that, he had taken his eye off the ball. That's all it was. It damn sure wasn't his fault.

And it definitely wasn't because WCW was a more capable promotion. Their shows weren't even close to being as good as the WWF's.

Were they?

And the WWF characters that fans were mocking. It was just a few select smart marks who hated them.

Wasn't it?

And Hogan and Savage . . . the guys McMahon had sent out to pasture . . . the ones WCW was now using as main-eventers. There was no way Vince had miscalculated their value.

Had he?

Hell no. No, he had not. This was *not* his fault.

But what about this Bischoff guy giving away *Raw*'s results? How was that fair? Who was Bischoff, anyway? Some smug little prick whom Vince hadn't even acknowledged when he auditioned for a job with the WWF years ago.

Well, the last thing Vince would do would be to acknowledge Bischoff now. But he sure as hell would acknowledge that Turner, a huge media conglomerate, was using illegal tactics to try and drive McMahon's poor little mom-and-pop company into bankruptcy. Because, really, that's the only way anyone could compete with Vince. Illegally. That's how Vince saw it.

Besides, even if Turner wasn't using illegal tactics, McMahon could become a huge pain in Bischoff's neck by simply implying that he was.

And so, in the opening months of 1996, Vince unveiled the "Billionaire Ted" skits, in which he mocked those in the Turner organization. The first few vignettes were humorous, featuring Billionaire Ted, the Huckster, the Nacho Man, and Scheme Gene sitting in the Wrestlin' Warroom, plotting the next WCW show. Some footage of high-flying WWF action was aired, and Ted asked his aging wrestlers to perform the same maneuvers. "At my age," the Huckster replied, "my feet don't leave the ground!" As is the case with any good parody, it was funny, if somewhat skewed. It looked at what WCW was presenting each week, and the message was clear: the WWF was presenting young, athletic main-eventers, while WCW was showcasing old guys living on their reputations.

The folks at Turner's headquarters more or less ignored the skits. Like a child desperate for attention, Vince became obsessed with getting under Turner's skin. The sketches moved away from wrestling and on to hot topics like WCW's lax steroid policy and Turner's political views. They became more and more personal, strongly alleging that Hogan was using illegal drugs and that Turner was a racist. At one point, they even made light of the death of Turner's father.

The WWF went so far as to buy ad space in national newspapers warning Turner stockholders that Ted had a personal vendetta against the WWF and was willing to lose millions every year in an attempt to put the McMahons out of business. Old-time wrestling fans scoffed at the idea of the McMahons being portrayed as victims in this game. It smacked of hypocrisy, as the WWF had used all kinds of questionable tactics against smaller organizations throughout the '80s, forcing the local promotions to shut their doors or attempt to compete with them by going national.

The only difference is that this time, it was Vince on the receiving end.

It was obvious that McMahon was simply trying to stir up trouble, especially since this was right about the time that Time Warner was talking of a merger with Turner. Certainly, Turner would shut down WCW before losing out on one of the biggest mergers of all time, right? That was the thinking, and a sign of just how desperate McMahon had become.

Turner's lawyers became involved, and the Billionaire Ted skits came to a merciful end. Bischoff wasn't happy about the skits, but, to his credit, he didn't stoop to Vince's level. Instead, he unveiled his master creation, the nWo. The angle went through the roof, leaving the WWF in WCW's dust.

And eventually, it turned WCW itself into dust.

nWoverkill

During the first year or so of the famed Monday Night Wars between *Nitro* and *Raw*, things were virtually dead even. Hulk Hogan and his band of WWF outcasts had made WCW competitive, but they alone could not topple the WWF in the ratings or in the minds of most wrestling fans. However, once WWF star after WWF star began migrating to WCW, the audience took note. Every week, someone else from the WWF was showing up on *Nitro*.

Eric Bischoff noticed how the fans were picking up on this and decided that he could build an angle from it. He had studied a promotional war that had taken place in Japan years ago, and he thought such an angle might be successful in the U.S. as well. This logic was backed up by the WWF's Jim Cornette, who said that the only thing wrestling fans really believed anymore was that the WWF and WCW hated each other.

When Kevin Nash and Scott Hall made their entrance to WCW, they announced that they had come not to win a championship or to knock off any particular foe. Instead, they were coming to destroy the company. Period. "You want a war?" Hall asked during his first WCW interview. "We'll give you a war." WCW didn't even identify Hall or Nash by name, although both still looked pretty much like their WWF personas of Razor Ramon and Diesel. Though no one ever came out and said it, the intent was obvious: the WWF wanted to invade WCW through Hall and Nash.

At *Bash at the Beach '96*, a mysterious third man was added to the group . . . Hulk Hogan. Hogan spit on the fans, claiming that they hadn't treated him with the respect he deserved since his arrival in WCW. Apparently he felt he deserved respect for pushing his friends into main events and bringing back Zeus. He claimed that he, Hall, and Nash were the New World Order of wrestling and were going to tear down WCW brick by brick. The nWo name stuck, and it was instantly the talk of the wrestling world.

Week by week, more WWF refugees joined the nWo. And it wasn't hacks like Repo Man or El Matador, but rather the few guys the WWF still had under contract that fans took seriously. Ted DiBiase, Sean Waltman, and others quickly joined. The nWo even brought in longtime WWF jobber Mike Jones, aka Virgil, Ted DiBiase's manservant in the WWF. WCW dubbed Jones "Vincent," as in Vince McMahon — which is pretty ironic, considering that Virgil was originally named Virgil as a shot at Virgil Runnels, who worked for WCW as Dusty Rhodes. Wrestling's petty like that. Promoters don't like someone, so they create a character or angle that makes no sense and has no hope of drawing money just to piss on someone. The mature wrestling promoter is a rare beast indeed.

McMahon was furious about the nWo angle. It wasn't because someone had come up with a creative angle. They hadn't. Oh, the fans might have thought it was creative, and maybe they were even buying tickets to WCW events, but it was far from creative. WCW was just tricking the fans into think that the WWF was invading, because that is the only way WCW could draw. It was because of the WWF that WCW was beating the WWF. That had to be it!

The WWF filed a lawsuit claiming just that. To rebut, Bischoff asked Hall point-blank, on camera, if he was still in the employ of the WWF. Hall said no. There could be no confusion now. They were the New World Order, not the WWF. They weren't Razor Ramon and Diesel; they were Scott Hall and Kevin Nash.

Not good enough! McMahon cried foul again, claiming that Hall and Nash might be calling themselves Hall and Nash, but they were really still playing the parts of Razor and Diesel, characters that the WWF had created. After all, Scott Hall was still throwing his toothpick at the screen, just like Razor had done, and Nash wore a similar black outfit to Diesel's. It never occurred to McMahon that Hall actually threw toothpicks during his first stint in WCW as the Diamond Studd. Or that black was a fairly common color. While McMahon didn't pick up on these facts, a judge did, and the trial was in limbo for years.

The lawsuit having failed him, McMahon decided to try other avenues to break the nWo's ratings stranglehold, even if only for a week. He was so desperate, in fact, that he was willing to bait and switch the loyal fans he had left, leading to one of the single dumbest angles in the history of the company.

In order to accomplish this goal, McMahon used one of the few men in the company who had any credibility left with fans: *Raw*'s lead announcer, Jim Ross. Ross began to state that he was hearing through the rumor mill that Diesel and Razor Ramon were on their way back to the WWF. Everyone inside both the WWF and WCW were confused as to how this could be, as Hall and Nash had just signed multiyear deals with Turner.

Despite the fact that virtually no one was buying it, Ross continued telling the WWF's rapidly diminishing audience that Razor and Diesel were coming back. Glimpses of Ramon and Diesel were shown on WWF television. After a few weeks of this, Ross not only reiterated his story, but he also gave an exact date for their return: September 23, 1996. It would be a live broadcast, and McMahon just knew the entire wrestling world was curious as to exactly what was going to happen.

After teasing their appearance for the entire night, Jim Ross entered the ring during the last segment of the show. He began to talk about how no one believed him when he said that Razor and Diesel were returning. He then segued into how he, Jim Ross, had been shafted time and again by Vince McMahon and the WWF. He went into great detail about how he was fired by the company a few years earlier following his diagnosis with Bell's palsy, a disease that had paralyzed half of his face.

Following his tirade against the company he worked for, Ross brought out Razor Ramon. Desperate to believe that Razor had come back, the crowd cheered upon hearing the Latin rhythm and squealing tires of his entrance theme. It had been too long since they had heard it. The roar of the crowd quickly died, however, when "Razor" came down the ramp.

This was not the Razor they remembered. This was not Scott Hall. This was a fake.

It was an indy worker by the name of Rick Bogner who was given the unenviable task of duplicating Scott Hall's WWF act. Bogner did somewhat resemble Hall in that he was tanned and had black hair. Bogner did not resemble Hall in that he was at least six inches shorter and had a bit of a gut. His partner in crime was Glen Jacobs, portraying Diesel. For Jacobs, this was a definite step in the right direction. He may have been booed out of the building, but at least he was being booed as an actual wrestler rather than as his former persona of evil dentist Isaac Yankem, DDS.

The crowd became unruly, chanting "fake, fake, fake!" at Ross's tandem. It was just what the WWF wanted — the spectators hated these two with a passion. Surely, fans would want to see these two impostors get their just licks. And hey, even if the WWF did annoy a few fans with this shady little game, McMahon could take comfort in knowing that the ratings for that evening were on his side. Yes, he may have alienated a handful of his most loyal supporters, but the ratings the next day would soften that blow.

Final score in the ratings: 3.4 to 2.0.

Raw was the 2.0.

It was one of the most lopsided contests since *Raw* and *Nitro* had gone head-to-head. McMahon was embarrassed again.

A rumor was quickly started that the idea for the fake angle wasn't to make money. Rather, the reason the WWF did something that insulted the intelligence of fans the world over was to prove that the characters they had created for Hall and Nash in the WWF were now of no use to the WWF. McMahon asserted that the way WCW used Hall and Nash had fans believing that they were the only true Razor and Diesel, and that no one else could play the roles. Once again, poor old Vince McMahon was getting shafted by the evil Turner empire.

Wrestling fans scoffed at this. They weren't the only ones. Eric Bischoff had a good, long laugh as well. This so-called Monday Night War wasn't a war at all. This was a one-sided joke.

And who could argue with Bischoff? The fans completely bought into the nWo angle. *Nitro* was plastering *Raw* in the ratings. This surge in popularity, combined with the WWF's complete ineptitude at the time, caused Bischoff to believe that WCW was invincible. He told his employees he believed that the WWF had less than a year to live. The small handful of talent they still had, such as Bret Hart, would soon be under WCW contract. With all their main-eventers working in WCW, Vince would have no recourse but to close up shop.

Yes, Bischoff was on top of the world. Magazines wanted to talk to this new czar of wrestling. Who cared what McMahon had to say? He was yesterday's news. Besides, Bischoff was a much better interview. While McMahon would talk in only vague terms about his competition, Bischoff would gloat about not even bothering to look at the ratings. He claimed that Vince McMahon was a fossil, and that WCW was the new number one. He may have crowed about WCW being better than the WWF before, but now he had the numbers to back it up.

One of Bischoff's more interesting claims was that he felt the nWo would be around forever. He certainly planned to make that so. After all, the angle put WCW over the top, and Bischoff felt as though it could easily stand the test of time. With the addition of Hulk Hogan to the mix, it gave the organization a sense of legitimacy that it had otherwise lacked.

And while the nWo was nothing more than a story line for WCW, the nWo had, in many ways, become superior to WCW. The nWo shirts sold far better than the WCW ones. Segments featuring the nWo were the highest rated on the telecasts. The nWo wrestlers generally won the matches, and most *Nitro* broadcasts ended with the WCW group facedown on the mat. Everyone wanted to be nWo, even Bischoff himself, who went so far as to write himself into story lines as the group's evil ringleader.

There was one man, however, who was the embodiment of WCW: Sting. As the "franchise player" of the company, he was a natural adversary of the nWo, and fans believed he was actually on the same level as Hogan, Hall, and Nash. He was therefore given a story line in which he watched from the rafters, waiting for just the right moment to strike at them, and specifically at Hogan and the world title. WCW wisely gave the feud plenty of time to simmer, waiting almost a year to deliver the epic match. Ratings for *Nitro* escalated to unheard-of levels, reaching nearly 5.0. Finally, with fans salivating for the showdown like Pavlov's dogs, Hogan vs. Sting was announced for *Starrcade '97.*

Anyone with a brain knew what the finish would be: Sting pummeling Hogan, destroying him en route to the world title. It only made sense, as Sting had been chasing Hogan for twelve long months. Anything else would be counterproductive to WCW's long-term well-being.

Hogan, though, had other plans. After once again being the center of attention, he had little desire to be shunted back down the card. Therefore, a plan was set in place wherein Hogan would actually pin Sting in the middle of the ring with a fast count from an evil referee. The match would be restarted, at which point Sting would defy all odds and win the belt. It wasn't the clean win fans would be expecting, but at least it would have cemented Sting as the champion and humiliated the nWo.

So, of course, that didn't happen. Instead, the evil referee's "fast count" had a normal cadence, possibly even a bit slow, making it look as though Sting had just blown his opportunity. (Whether this was planned ahead of time or whether Hogan got in the ref's ear prior to the match is up for debate.) The match was restarted and Sting won the belt as planned, but the damage was done.

Still, Sting had the belt.

For about a week.

The belt was suspended due to the controversy surrounding the title match. While Sting did eventually win the belt, he dropped it again just weeks later. The belt wound up back in the camp of the nWo, and eventually back to Hogan himself. After over a year of buildup, Sting was sent back down the card.

Sting was portrayed as a loser. So were the rest of the WCW "good guys." For years, they couldn't compare to the WWF, and now their own company was making sure WCW couldn't measure up to the New World Order. The nWo went to great lengths to illustrate that point, not just by pummeling the WCW wrestlers, but also by telling fans flat out that WCW sucked.

Remember that the nWo were the heels in the story. That's very important, and often overlooked. Here you had the bad guys, who beat up fan favorites week after week, telling those same WCW fans that the product that they had purchased tickets to or had watched on TV was horrible.

This led to a legitimate concern among the wrestlers backstage. No one in the locker room wanted to be part of Team WCW. For the boys in the back, it made no sense financially to be members of a group that was made out to be a bunch of pathetic losers. As members of the nWo, they would have more visibility on TV, and would be on the winning end of things more often than not. This increased exposure would give them better merchandising sales and, therefore, more money in their pockets.

After seeing how the main hero of WCW was booked, virtually everyone in the back wanted to be in the nWo. Of course, if everyone was a bad guy, it didn't make for much of a story. That didn't keep the company from turning this legitimate backstage paranoia into an angle, as the nWo started a "membership drive." The nWo drew a line in the sand; you were either with them or against them.

Keep in mind that, to this point, the group had been comprised solely of major stars in the business. Hall and Nash were both headliners in the WWF; Hogan was the single biggest name in wrestling in the past 20 years. The other new recruits may not have been quite that famous, but fans still knew them from their stints in the WWF.

Suddenly, though, no names were joining the group. It was one thing for Ted DiBiase to be added to the crew. He had main-evented for the WWF as the Million Dollar Man. It was another for Marcus Bagwell to join. He had main-evented . . . well, never. He just happened to be in the right place at the right time. The same thing happened over and over and over again. Guys like Stevie Ray, who had achieved some level of fame as half of the tag team Harlem Heat, was given a push. The problem is that he wasn't very good in the ring and had little charisma outside it. This type of thing really watered down the entire nWo concept.

Hogan was smart, though. He saw what was happening and didn't want the nWo to be pulled down by it. This was likely his last chance at stardom. He remembered the ratings and the buy rates before the nWo. He also remembered how many within the company wanted him to step aside. Not now. Now he was again the center of attention, back where he belonged. The last thing he would let the bookers do was yank away his spotlight.

Thus, the first cracks in the nWo became apparent, and the group was splintered. Hogan, Hall, and Nash remained the focal point, while the so-called B-Team, consisting of the likes of Bagwell and Ray, was given menial tasks to do.

Like destroying the *Nitro* set.

When the ratings were hitting their zenith, serious thought was given to making a show that was solely about the nWo. Not just any show, mind you, but the flagship of WCW itself, *Nitro*. The thinking was that since fans tuned in more for the nWo than for any other segments, an entire show based on the group would be a surefire hit. Of course, if the whole show was on around the group, who would they fight? Themselves?

That didn't stop WCW from trying it out, though. The inaugural nWo *Nitro* featured the makeshift announce squad of Bischoff, Nash, and Rick

Rude making fun of WCW wrestlers and kissing each other's asses. Nearly 20 minutes of the show revolved around the group giving Christmas gifts to Hulk Hogan as Bischoff warbled "White Christmas." It was just like *The Osmond Family Christmas*. . . if Marie had been hepped up on goofballs and Donny was suffering from 'roid rage.

Not only was it horrendous TV, but it also ate up valuable time, as this show went head-to-head with *Raw*. Almost 30 minutes was allotted to showing the nWo tearing down every banner and sign featuring the WCW insignia. If you ever wanted to see how a wrestling set gets torn down after the final bell rings and the crowd heads home, then this was the show for you!

But no one wanted to see that. The ratings proved it, as the show dropped a full half point, drawing the smallest audience in almost four months. The format for the show was scrapped, and nWo *Nitro* was never spoken of again.

The company really should have known better, as they had attempted to cash in on the nWo's popularity with a pay-per-view earlier in the year: *Souled Out '97*. The event was certainly unique, featuring a bizarre black-and-white set with neo-Nazi style imagery. WCW was once again made to look like the fool, as the good guys were ridiculed not only by the heel announcers, but during ring introductions as well. The show featured a grotesque "beauty contest," with biker chicks so hideous they likely would have been rejected from *Hustler's* "Beaver Hunt."

Souled Out '97 was a flop. That didn't matter to Bischoff, who had become obsessed with ensuring that the nWo — his creation — overshadowed everything else in the promotion. Even wrestlers who weren't nWo were placed in other groups that were *like* the nWo.

Groups like nWo Japan. One of the main differences between the early days of *Nitro* and the early days of *Raw* was that Bischoff had the foresight to give fans some of the best actual wrestling action available on the planet. He did this by importing outstanding grapplers from all over the world. The most technically sound wrestlers of the era were generally either from Mexico or Japan, where wrestling is considered more of an art form. Masahiro Chono and the Great Muta were brought in as the cornerstones for nWo Japan, since the booking committee felt that they couldn't get over based on their in-ring skills alone.

In addition to the Japanese stars, Bischoff also signed several stars from Mexico, where a style known as *lucha libre* was king. *Lucha libre* is a much more athletic, high-flying style of wrestling than what Americans were used to seeing. After bringing in such sensations as Rey Mysterio Jr. and Juventud Guerrera, they decided to put them into their own nWo-style organization. And thus the lWo, or Latino World Order, was born.

Even the groups who fought the nWo were designed with the template Bischoff had created. When the Ultimate Warrior was brought in to help boost ratings, he created his own army, the oWn: One Warrior Nation. See, it was like the nWo but in reverse. How clever. That the group consisted of only the Warrior and Ed Leslie (wouldn't that have made it a Two Warrior Nation?) didn't matter. What did matter was the tie-in to Bischoff's creation.

This was all getting a bit silly, and fans were really starting to tire of it. The biggest issue, of course, was that no matter who they fought, the original group never lost. Much of this was due to backstage politics; Hogan and Nash, specifically, were good friends with Bischoff, whom they played like a fiddle. Main events therefore featured wrestlers Bischoff liked rather than those whom the fans wanted to see.

Case in point: Diamond Dallas Page. Dallas Page was nothing more than a midcarder before Bischoff took the reigns. In fact, his most notable feud was with Evad Sullivan in an angle that consisted of arm wrestling, dyslexia, and rabbit stew.

No, seriously.

In the spring of 1995, Page got his first big break, and it just happened to be at about the time that Bischoff came into power. DDP began challenging other wrestlers to arm wrestling contests, billing himself as the "International Big-Arm Arm Wrestling Champion." He even carried a trophy to the ring to verify this completely bogus accomplishment. His bouts had a special stipulation: if Page were defeated, his valet, Kimberly, would go on a date with the winner.

Evad Sullivan entered the fray to confront Page. This set up pro wrestling cliché #373: idiotic wrestler falls in puppy love with beautiful girl who just so happens to manage nefarious villain. In this instance, Evad was injured during a bout, and Kimberly, being the kind soul she was, visited him in the hospital. She brought him a gift—a rabbit. Evad named the rabbit Ralph, and promised to hug him and squeeze him and pet him and pet him on account of he loved him so very much.

Upon his release from the hospital, Evad tracked down Page. The arm wrestling showdown between the two came with an added stipulation: if DDP won, he would get to put Ralph in a stew. After training on a playground with a bunch of seven year olds, Evad beat DDP and won the date. Page, wearing a bunny suit, attacked Evad during his night on the town with Kimberly. Somehow, this restored DDP's confidence, and he dominated Evad for the remainder of the feud.

How beating an idiot like Evad Sullivan night after night was supposed to be material upon which to base a championship career is anyone's guess, but three years later, Diamond Dallas Page had traded in the rabbit suit for the top belt in the promotion. It can certainly be argued that Page worked hard to improve as a wrestler; indeed, through sheer determination, he became one of the company's better grapplers. However, others within the company worked just as hard and were more marketable to boot. It's hard to imagine him getting the world title without being a member of Bischoff's posse.

Although keeping his friends happy was a main concern, Bischoff also fancied himself as something more than a wrestling promoter. He loved to rub elbows with celebrities, and he spared no expense to bring in those who had made names for themselves in mainstream entertainment. Bischoff not only wanted the publicity these stars would bring to his company, but he also wanted to make a name for himself outside the wrestling business.

Bischoff initially dabbled with legitimate sports figures, many of whom were intrigued by the pro wrestling scene. Basketball players such as Dennis Rodman and Karl Malone were drawn to the ring by the promise of huge paydays, and, to be fair, the ratings and buy rates sometimes validated the spending. The problem was, of course, that the NBA stars really didn't have time to train properly for the events. Despite their natural abilities, it was amateur hour when they stepped through the ropes. Still, it was all worth it just to hear Rodman introduced by Michael Buffer, another celebrity Bischoff had hired: "His fierce competitiveness and desire to win has earned him the label of 'bad boy,' and he's proud of it. Because he's so good, he's as baaaaaaad as he wants to be. And that's very, very bad. Ladies and gentleman, the ultimate bad boy, Dennis Rodman!"

Just in case wrestling fans didn't grasp the subtle notion that Rodman was "bad," he got in the ring and proved it. He wasn't just bad, he was hideous. And it wasn't just due to his inadequate training; "The Worm" viewed WCW shows as an excuse to party, and he would arrive in no shape to perform. You could almost say he was confronting his personal demons.

At least bringing in athletes gave WCW a sense of legitimacy. That wasn't the case when Jay Leno made his in-ring debut.

Yes, *that* Jay Leno.

This angle began when Bischoff started his own talk show on *Nitro* telecasts, "nWo Nightcap." He sat behind a desk that looked eerily like the one on the *Tonight Show* set. He told jokes to canned laughter, often stealing gags that Leno himself had used on his show days prior. The segments were designed to annoy fans, and since they ranged up to 20 minutes in length, they accomplished their mission. Fans sitting in the audience at live WCW shows were incensed by the skits; those at home simply flipped the channel to *Raw*. Few angles illustrate the difference between good heat, which generates money, and bad heat, which inspires fans to vow never to watch a show again, better than this one.

The angle was successful in generating mainstream publicity, however. Leno made reference to the nWo during his *Tonight Show* monologues, which were seen by a far greater audience than *Nitro*. A match was eventually signed with Bischoff and Hulk Hogan against Leno and DDP for *Road Wild '98*.

Ah, *Road Wild*. The event was originally called *Hogg Wild*, and it was WCW's August pay-per-view. It took place in Sturgis, South Dakota, during the annual biker rally, which was a great excuse for Bischoff, a huge motorcycle enthusiast, to make the trek. WCW would set up a ring in the middle of a field, and hardcore bikers would surround the ring with their rides, revving up their engines when they saw something they liked.

Aside from the fact that WCW made nothing in terms of live gate for the show, a major issue with the event was that most bikers knew nothing about the wrestling product. The few that did were either too drunk or stoned to really comprehend what was happening in the ring, and they would cheer whomever they thought looked cool. It didn't matter if they were face or heel, nor what the story line was leading to the match. This reached a preposterous level during the 1996 version of the event, in which Dean Malenko and Chris Benoit put on a technical classic that the crowd nearly booed out of the ring.

With this in mind, maybe it *was* a good idea for WCW to present Jay Leno's first match to this type of crowd. Despite looking completely out of place among the chiseled physiques in the ring, Leno performed a handful of simplistic moves and emerged the victor. The match was a complete farce, an affront to every man or woman who ever trained to be a wrestler.

It made sense that Leno was worse than Rodman, because Rodman was an athlete. Another celebrity WCW brought in was worse than Leno, because Leno was a human.

For several weeks during the summer of 1998, howling laughter filled *Nitro* arenas. No one knew where this evil laughter was coming from, nor did they know who it was that had the giggles. Week after week, the mystery went unsolved. The culprit was finally revealed during an interview with Rick Steiner, as a familiar face filled the video wall. It was Chucky, the stitched-up doll from the *Child's Play* horror films. He had begun to promote his new film, *Bride of Chucky*, when Steiner told the puppet to bring his "raggedy rear end down to the ring!" Yes, Rick Steiner actually challenged a doll to a match. Someone actually thought this was a good idea for both WCW and the movie.

It wasn't like WCW hadn't been through a fiasco like this before. In 1990, WCW did some cross-promotion for the movie *Robocop 2*; in fact, their *Capital Combat* pay-per-view was subtitled *Return of Robocop*. Robocop himself was to be at the event live, to make sure that the bad guys played by the rules. They didn't, of course—they locked Sting into a small cage. Robocop lumbered to ringside, pulled the "iron" bars from their hinges, and then just as slowly lumbered to the back. Keep in mind that months had been spent promoting his appearance, and it lasted little more than two or three minutes.

At least Robocop made sense. It was possible that the movie hero could, somehow, some way, give a rub to Sting. There can be no explanation, however, for WCW's decision in the mid-1990s to bring in psychic guru Gary Spivey to give pep talks to a down-on-his-luck Paul Orndorff. The former Mr. Wonderful, who was a huge star for the WWF and had main-evented with Hulk Hogan, had begun to doubt himself and his abilities. Just as things looked most bleak, Spivey walked into Orndorff's locker room, prompting the following dialogue:

Orndorff: "Gary Spivey! From the Psychic Companions Network? What are you doing here?"

Spivey: "I got a vision. I knew you weren't OK."

Orndorff: "You did? How?"

Spivey: "I got a vision. Psychics know!"

Spivey, whose head of hair resembled a giant SOS pad, convinced Orndorff that he really was worthy of the Mr. Wonderful moniker. Orndorff, no doubt inspired by this pep talk, retired two months later.

Bischoff, having forgotten these and other past celebrity disasters, appeared to go insane following the Leno experiment, bringing in any celebrity he could find. He even signed a million-dollar deal with Gene Simmons to create a wrestler based on his heavy metal band. Alas, the KISS Demon went nowhere.

Eventually, Bischoff ran out of folks willing to deal with the promotion and was forced to drop to lesser-known figures, ranging from rap artist Master P to Will Sasso from *Mad TV*. As each celebrity who passed through the doors was less and less a "celebrity," fans ceased to care.

Which was becoming the case with WCW as a whole. The celebrities weren't changing the fact that the main story line of the promotion — nWo versus WCW — had been beaten into the ground. The nWo had beaten WCW so many times that fans no longer believed that WCW was an organization worth supporting. WCW were losers. The nWo told fans that, and had proved it time and time again. And if the nWo had no competition, what was the point of paying to see them? Ratings began to free-fall as expenses skyrocketed. Even when notable WWF performers such as Bret Hart jumped shipped, fans were disinterested. They had seen it all before. The nWo beats WCW. Yawn.

With WCW in a shambles, *Raw* began to beat *Nitro* in the weekly ratings. Just as it looked as though the gravy train had reached its end, out of nowhere came one last hope: Bill Goldberg. A powerhouse who rarely spoke, Goldberg caught fans' eyes as he obliterated every opponent in his path. It appeared that no one could stop him as he racked up win after win, eventually compiling a record of over 100 wins without a single loss. Fans truly believed that this was the man who could stop the reign of terror of the nWo.

Shockingly, Hulk Hogan agreed to drop his WCW title to Goldberg. The match was set to take place at *Nitro* in WCW's backyard, the Georgia Dome in Atlanta, in July of 1998. It was interesting, because in the weeks leading up to the show, the match was scheduled to be a nontitle and nontelevised encounter. Therefore, Hogan could lose the match without fans at home knowing and without losing the strap. Within a week of the match, however, WCW changed it to a title match that would be televised live on *Nitro* in the hopes that they could derail *Raw*'s momentum.

As planned, Hogan lost the belt to Goldberg. The match was a ratings success, drawing the highest ratings in the history of cable wrestling to that point. WCW celebrated, as the Goldberg-Hogan match enabled *Nitro* to once again beat *Raw* in the ratings, if only for that one week.

One can only guess how huge the buy rate of the first-ever Goldberg vs. Hogan title match might have been. Instead, WCW flushed that all away in hopes of stopping *Raw*'s winning streak. Millions of dollars down the drain, just for a chance at a one-week ratings spike. And that was generally what it amounted to, as Raw was usually on top once again the following week. This happened all the time, as WCW was so desperate to regain control of the ratings that they would give away for free what people would gladly have paid to seen on pay-per-view. In the wrestling business, that's called *hotshotting*.

WCW made an art form of it as 1998 came to a close. Every possible high-profile main event was given away free on *Nitro*, which was great for short-term ratings, but tanked pay-per-view buy rates, which is where the company really made its money. Having given away every possible high-profile main event for free on *Nitro*, WCW's ratings again began to drop.

Still, with Goldberg as champion, fans saw a glimmer of hope. It wasn't meant to last, as backstage politicians such as Hogan and Nash were undermining Goldberg's title reign. To ensure Goldberg's failure as champion, he was never given credible opponents. The few men who fans would have viewed as viable contenders simply wouldn't allow themselves to become the latest victim of the streak. Therefore, Goldberg was given jobber after jobber, each of them presented as a so-called "number-one contender." Hogan maintained his high-profile presence on the show with a bogus run for the United States presidency. With no one else on the roster willing to face Goldberg, Nash was dubbed the number-one contender.

And why did Nash allow himself to become the top contender? Because he just so happened to be in charge of the creative team at the time. What a co-inky-dink. Therefore, at *Starrcade*, the biggest show of the year, Kevin Nash defeated Goldberg, taking the title and ending Goldberg's undefeated streak at 172-0. Nash and Hogan convinced Bischoff that Goldberg's title reign was a complete disaster, and that Goldberg himself was the real cause for the ratings fall-off. Goldberg, the man fans believed could be a real opponent for the nWo, was moved down the card to flounder without any real focus.

With Goldberg safely buried in the midcard, Hogan and Nash kept the spotlight on the nWo, splitting the group in two: nWo Hollywood, led by Hogan, and nWo Wolfpac, headed up by Nash. This focused the shows entirely on the nWo. Never mind the fact that fans had already become bored with them, nor that this continued the trend of making WCW look like a bunch of losers. This set up what Nash and Hogan wanted all along: Hogan vs. Nash as the marquee matchup in the company.

Once more, instead of saving this for a pay-per-view, WCW rushed the match to air on the first *Nitro* of 1999, again emanating from Atlanta. With 40,000 strong on hand to witness the showdown, WCW made yet another tactical error. *Raw* had been pretaped, and, therefore, the results of the WWF matches weren't exactly a secret. On this night, Mankind (Mick Foley), a fan favorite on *Raw* who had been picking up steam, was about to make it to the top of the mountain. Bischoff, through a headset, instructed *Nitro* announcer Tony Schiavone to mock the WWF with the following announcement: "Fans, if you're even thinking about changing the channel to our competition, do not. We understand that Mick Foley, who wrestled here one time as Cactus Jack, is gonna win their World title. Ha ha! That's gonna put some butts in the seats!"

Immediately upon hearing this, nearly half a million viewers switched from *Nitro* to *Raw*.

And what of the Hogan-Nash main event? The bell sounded as *Nitro's* three-hour window was about to close. Nash ripped his shirt in a manner that mocked Hogan. The two men circled each other, and the crowd was on the edge of their seats. Schiavone proclaimed, "This is what pro wrestling, this is what World Championship Wrestling, is all about."

Little did he know just how right he was. Nash shoved Hogan. Hogan retaliated by drawing back his fist then lightly poking his finger in Nash's chest. Nash fell to the mat as though he'd been hit by a cannonball. Hogan covered him for the 1-2-3 and was once again the heavyweight champion of the world. Nash hopped up and handed Hogan the belt as both nWo Wolfpac and nWo Hollywood ran in to celebrate. Goldberg came out to demolish the group, but he was beaten down and spray painted with the nWo logo. Just like Sting almost two years before to the day, Goldberg was made out to be a total loser.

Hogan and Nash had duped the fans again. The nWo was really all the show was ever about.

You see, the reason Hogan agreed to lose to Goldberg in the first place was so that he could be the one to end the streak. But he allowed Nash to defeat Goldberg in return for getting the title back. And since Nash didn't want to job the belt in a real match, he would drop the belt without a fight. The end result saw Hogan and Nash on top, the WCW title devalued, and Goldberg buried.

The crowd didn't care about the backstage shenanigans. They booed the segment mercilessly. Fans at home, upon hearing that Foley was about to win the world title from the Rock, immediately switched the channel.

The head-to-head title matches saw Rock-Foley with a 5.9, versus Nash-Hogan with a 4.6. This gave *Raw* not only its largest rating ever to that point, but also enabled it to handily beat *Nitro* that evening.

And that was that. Fans had been burned one time too many by WCW and the nWo. From that point on in 1999, ratings steadily dropped for the company as it kept trying to relive its past glory by shoving the nWo down fans' throats. On January 4, 1999, *Nitro* scored a 5.01 rating. By the end of the year, that would drop to under 3.0.

The nWo was dead. Fans no longer wanted to see Hogan, Nash, and the rest run roughshod over the WCW. They had seen it enough.

And the fans knew that WCW sucked.

After all, WCW had told them that themselves.

10

Sex as a Weapon

When WCW struck gold with the initial nWo invasion, the WWF wasn't quite sure how to counter. It appeared as though the WWF had invaded WCW via Nash and Hall, and fans were much more interested in what was happening on *Nitro* than on *Raw*. Add to this the fact that all of the WWF's top talent was fleeing the promotion as though the *Titanic* had just hit the iceberg, and it is no wonder that the company's status as the country's number-one wrestling promotion had vanished.

McMahon was reeling. His competitor had a seemingly endless supply of cash and appeared intent on driving his poor, family-owned business under. As if that weren't bad enough, his company was in complete disarray behind the scenes. Fights broke out between wrestlers, who had become frustrated watching their friends leave the Federation and make twice as much with Turner.

With the advent of the nWo, the WWF's *Monday Night Raw* was getting clobbered in the ratings. What could they do to compete? How could the WWF possibly stop this massacre?

Then someone hit upon a brilliant idea: what if they had a promotional war of their own? After all, WCW was offering a mock promotional war. What if the WWF created a real promotional war? With this thought, McMahon made an arrangement with the National Wrestling Alliance.

Whoa whoa whoa, you're no doubt saying. Wasn't the NWA part of WCW? It was. Then it wasn't. Ted Turner had bought the rights for the NWA from Jim Crockett to promote a show using his wrestlers. Crockett was a member of the NWA, but he was just one member. After several years of using the NWA belts and name, Turner officials simply decided to stop paying dues to the organization and begin promoting their company as World Championship Wrestling.

NWA officials were furious at the snub and went out to create a show of their own. However, with all their talent under contract to Turner, that was kind of tough to do. Though they did promote shows throughout the eastern United States, most fans viewed them as nothing more than another independent organization. Without a national television deal, it was a point that was hard to argue.

McMahon was desperate, however, and he forged a deal with Dennis Coralluzzo, the head of the NWA. The NWA belt was brought into the promotion, and promoted as an "old school" championship. It was immediately won by Jeff Jarrett. Fans didn't care, because this was the same Jeff Jarrett they had been watching for years, only now he had a shiny belt that only the most hardcore fan even recognized. And that was really all the NWA had to offer—a belt. They had no big names that fans would buy tickets to see.

The lack of big names was certainly beginning to hurt McMahon, especially as more of his talent was heading to Atlanta. The initial talent departures from the WWF included Kevin Nash, Scott Hall, Ted DiBiase, Sean Waltman (known as Syxx or X-Pac), Curt Hennig, and countless other lesser players. It seemed as if every week McMahon was losing another one of his top stars.

It wasn't a one-way street, however. There were those within WCW who hated what was going on in the company and were looking for any way possible to get out. Others had been fired. During the mid-to-late '90s, the WWF was able to sign three men for whom WCW had little use: Paul Levesque, Mick Foley, and Steve Austin. Many within the wrestling industry simply shook their heads at McMahon. While WCW's newly acquired workers were all well known to wrestling fans, none of the WWF's new recruits had any kind of name value. It was as if McMahon had just purchased a sack of magic beans.

In reality, he had. While most of the workers who had left the Federation were past their prime, McMahon's new recruits were younger and more athletic. They were also hungry, looking for a chance to prove that their former employer was foolish for letting them go. They just needed decent personas to help them accomplish that goal.

They didn't get them. At least, not at first. Paul Levesque had been through several identity changes in WCW. He began as a wildman known as Terra Ryzin. Yes, like "terrorizing." Shockingly, that flopped. WCW then retrofitted him as French royal Jean Paul Levesque. It wasn't much better, but it was a start, and he did what he could with it. WCW began to like what they were seeing and offered to sign Levesque to a new deal in which he would team with another snoot, Lord Steven Regal. Levesque refused, wanting a run as a singles competitor. WCW vetoed the request, so he headed to the WWF.

McMahon thought Levesque had a great deal of talent. As he was apt to do, McMahon patterned his new character on something that had happened to him in real life. The WWF head had just purchased a home in Greenwich, Connecticut, in an area of town populated by old money. McMahon felt his neighbors looked down upon him, due to the fact that he promoted such lowbrow entertainment. As a way of exacting revenge, Levesque was made to parody these elitists as the American blueblood Hunter Hearst

Helmsley. And naturally he hailed from Greenwich, Connecticut.

Helmsley would speak to fans with his nose held high in the air, ridiculing them for their appearance. Fans didn't care, and they found him to be very dull. Helmsley floundered about the WWF midcard, trading a win for a loss against the likes of garbageman Duke "The Dumpster" Droese and pig farmer Henry O. Godwinn, known as HOG to his friends. Levesque, though, was no fool, and he quickly became friends with a powerful backstage group known as the Clique.

The Clique was a collection of wrestlers, headed up by Shawn Michaels and Kevin Nash, who had Vince McMahon's ear. By buddying up to McMahon, they were able to see their little crew move up the ranks and become main-eventers. They had no problem making each other look good, as in the end it was to the benefit of the Clique. However, they did have a problem with making others within the promotion shine for fear that they might lose their spots at the top of the card.

The Clique, for all its power, also became a bit full of itself and began to make mistakes. Though Kevin Nash was WWF champion, his title reign was a flop, drawing the smallest crowds the Federation had seen in years. Shawn Michaels was constantly at odds with any non-McMahon management. Scott Hall often arrived at shows drun——. . . er . . . confronting personal demons. In short, many within the company began to see the Clique as troublemakers. Suffice to say, it wasn't a sad day for many in the company when both Nash and Hall gave their notice. Their final performance within the WWF, however, landed Helmsley, the Clique's junior member, in hot water with McMahon.

It was a house show at New York's Madison Square Garden on May 19, 1996. Michaels and Nash had just competed in a cage match, with Michaels, the guy who was staying with the company, winning the bout. Suddenly, the two wrestlers "broke character" and hugged in the middle of the ring. They waved backstage, and Hall and Helmsley both came out as well. All four shared a group hug as a way of saying goodbye to their old friends.

Vince McMahon was not amused by this show of camaraderie. While there was nothing he could to Nash and Hall, and little he could do to Michaels, who was in the midst of a WWF title reign, he vented his anger on the one guy he could: Helmsley. Hunter was immediately put on a losing streak that lasted almost a full year, before finally being given a push as Shawn Michaels's lackey in a group known as D-Generation X. Shortly after the formation of the group, Michaels suffered an injury that would put him out of action for the next four years. McMahon, having invested so much promotion in DX, didn't want to pull the plug quite yet, so he gave Hunter a shot at being a main-eventer.

It didn't really work. While McMahon had forgiven Helmsley, and therefore began once again to book him as an unstoppable force, the fans still found him boring. It didn't matter, because McMahon was determined to make Helmsley a star at any cost, and he did everything he could to make that happen. Finally, after several character modifications, about twenty different entrance songs, and wins over just about every superstar the WWF had, Helmsley achieved fame as Triple H.

Helmsley wasn't the only guy brought in with a lame gimmick. Mick Foley was a hardcore legend who had been known his entire career as Cactus Jack. You remember him, right? The guy who had his ear torn off by Vader in Germany? He too made his way to the WWF, where Vince McMahon fitted him with a medieval-looking costume and named him Mason the Mutilator. Foley, mortified at the character, quickly suggested a handful of changes and asked that the character be dubbed Mankind. McMahon relented and came up with a story in which Foley was a tremendous classical pianist as a child. However, his parents felt he just wasn't quite good enough, so they threw him in the sewers with the rats. This warped him into Mankind, a deranged psychopath who would mangle his opponents then quietly rock in the corner to soft piano music.

Shockingly, the rat-raised pianist persona didn't get over. However, Foley's insane level of risk-taking did get the fans' attention, particularly after he took a fall off a 15-foot steel cage to the arena floor below. After that match, McMahon allowed Foley to turn babyface and start showing some of his real, off-the-wall humor. He clicked with fans, going on to become not only a main-event wrestler for the WWF, but also a *New York Times* best-selling author. His book, *Have a Nice Day!*, and its follow-up, *Foley Is Good*, detail the silliness involved in his own career, and they are required reading for any wrestling fan.

The most notable of the WCW rejects, though, was Steve Austin. Austin had worked his way up the WCW ranks as "Stunning" Steve after learning the trade in Texas in the World Class region. Despite never getting much notice from WCW bookers, Austin put forth his best effort nightly, working tremendous matches in both solo action and with his tag team partner "Flyin'" Brian Pillman as the Hollywood Blondes. Finally, he was rewarded for his years of dedication and hard work with the U.S. Title, a belt that was generally considered a stepping-stone to the world championship itself.

Once Hulk Hogan entered the promotion, though, Austin became an afterthought. An over-the-hill "Hacksaw" Jim Duggan, yet another Hogan ally, pinned "Stunning" Steve for the belt in less than 30 seconds. Austin's WCW career never recovered. Eric Bischoff explained to Steve that there wasn't much they could do with him; from a marketing standpoint, he was just a guy who came to the ring wearing black tights and boots. He was injured while on tour in Japan, and fired by FedEx package after four years with the promotion.

It wouldn't be the last the world would hear from him, though. Austin recovered from his injury and landed a job with the WWF. McMahon knew very little about the guy and didn't put much thought into his character, "The Ringmaster." Thankfully, he did not come to the ring wearing a giant top hat and yelling, "Hurry, hurry, step right up!" Instead, he was turned into a generic heel and was given Ted DiBiase as a manager to do all his talking for him.

Much like Foley, Austin hated this initial character. He was given little to do, and he was mired in a feud with supposed Puerto Rican legend Savio Vega until DiBiase left for WCW. Austin saw this as his chance to break out on his own and went to McMahon requesting a new persona. The creative department, who saw little in Austin, told him they didn't have time to do this, and if he wanted something else, he'd have to come up with it on his own. After watching a documentary on serial killers, Austin surmised that an interesting character could be based on that. He took the idea to creative, who were unimpressed, but they said they'd give it a shot, likely for no reason other than to get the guy to leave them alone.

Now all he needed was a name. Austin set out to find a moniker that conveyed the character's cold-blooded demeanor, and again he went to the creative department for ideas. They came back with several pages of names, one of which was Chilly McFreeze. *Chilly McFreeze!* What would he do, attack his victims with a popsicle?

Thankfully, Austin turned down their ideas and racked his brain. Luck was on his side, as his wife, Jeannie, had fixed him some hot tea. As Austin was about to beat his head against the wall, Jeannie, who was originally from England, warned him, "Drink your tea before it gets stone cold." That was it — he would become "Stone Cold" Steve Austin.

The name caught on with fans. Austin began to ratchet up the character several notches, using four-letter words and flipping the bird to fans and opponents alike. Such a thing had never really been done in wrestling, so the shock value alone was tremendous. McMahon saw the character starting to catch fire and advised Austin to do and say whatever he wanted. Fans began tuning in to see just how far he would push the envelope.

At the *King of the Ring* pay-per-view in 1996, Austin beat Jake Roberts in the tournament final. By this point in his career, Roberts had confronted his personal demons and become a religious man, often making reference to the Bible in his promos. Upon pinning Roberts, Austin took the stage, screaming, "You talk about your Psalms, you talk about your John 3:16 . . . Austin 3:16 says I just whipped your ass!"

McMahon couldn't make Austin 3:16 T-shirts fast enough. Foam hands, the kind that football fans use to say their team is number one, were modified so that the middle finger was extended. The ruder and more outlandish the promotion became, the more headway they made in the ratings war. Finally, with the help of boxer Mike Tyson and a heel turn by Vince McMahon himself, *Raw* overtook *Nitro* in the ratings.

McMahon now knew how to conquer WCW: crank up the raunch, then yank off the knob. Suddenly, Triple H was gesturing at his crotch and telling opponents to "Suck it!" and Austin was flipping off everyone in sight. McMahon told his wrestlers to be as obscene as the network would allow. In fact, a 1999 study by Indiana University researchers gives a pretty good indication of the vulgarity that the company used to achieve its ratings turnaround. The study covered 50 episodes of *Raw* from the 1998–'99 season. The results showed that a wrestler either grabbed or pointed to his crotch 1,658 times, said "Suck it!" 434 times, and made 157 middle-finger gestures.

Critics called it obscene. McMahon called it "Attitude."

The WWF pushed boundaries in many other ways as well. The company began to dabble in extreme violence, including the use of firearms in a showdown between Austin and former partner Brian Pillman. Pillman had been involved in a car wreck shortly before entering the WWF, and he was in need of surgery to repair the damage. Austin attacked his old friend in the ring, "breaking" his ankle. That wasn't enough for the bloodthirsty Rattlesnake, however, as he headed to Pillman's house in Kentucky before a live nationwide audience.

This time, however, Pillman was ready: he was packing heat. Announcer Kevin Kelly, stationed at Pillman's bedside, looked absolutely terrified; indeed, it appeared that he might wet his pants at any moment. Melanie Pillman, Brian's real-life wife, was bonkers as well. Throughout the *Raw* broadcast, scared WWF employees would call in to the show and give updates, acting as though this was a publicity stunt that had gotten completely out of control.

As Austin broke into Pillman's house, shots were fired, and the WWF suddenly "lost" the satellite feed. The Federation, leery of saying the word "gunshot," opted instead for "explosions." When the feed resumed, Pillman was screaming, "I'm going to kill that son of a bitch! I'm going to kill that motherfucker!"

While McMahon was reportedly elated with the skit, the USA Network, which aired *Raw*, was not. They warned McMahon that any more action like this could result in serious problems for the WWF. McMahon, though, knew that he was onto something and wasn't about to stop now. Who the hell cared if they were offending people? They were getting noticed, and that was what was important.

The race card was played as well, as the company threw together three ethnic groups and had them feud, the result being the infamous Gang Warz of 1997. This feud had everything a bigot could want, as white bikers, Puerto Ricans, and black militants worked out their aggression against each other in every type of match possible.

The motorcycle gang was known as Disciples of Apocalypse, or DOA for short. They were a skinhead group led by Crush, Brian Lee (Chainz), and a pair of identical twins named Ron (Skull) and Don (8-Ball) Harris. Despite having zero talent, the Harris brothers always seemed to have jobs in wrestling, seemingly changing gimmicks on a weekly basis. They were originally Appalachian Mountain men Jacob and Eli Blu, and then they became the Grimm Twins before settling in as Harley-riding hellraisers.

The only really interesting thing about the brothers — and this is only interesting in a perverse sense — was a plastic surgery that went awry. In 1996, Don underwent surgery to bolster his pectoral area. For lack of a better term, he had a boob job. A *manly* boob job, to be sure, but a boob job nonetheless. While examining his perky new breasts, Harris noticed something wrong — his nipple was off center. And not just by a little! Harris filed a lawsuit against the doctor, claiming that he was mortified every time he removed his shirt. Maybe wrestling fans can file a class action lawsuit claiming they are mortified every time he steps into the ring.

Feuding with the Wayward Nipple Motorcycle Gang were Los Boriquas, a foursome from Puerto Rico. The leader of the group was Savio Vega, who had wrestled under a mask as Kwang the Evil Ninja. Yes, a *Puerto Rican* ninja. Also in the group was Miguel Perez, who had so much body hair that fans

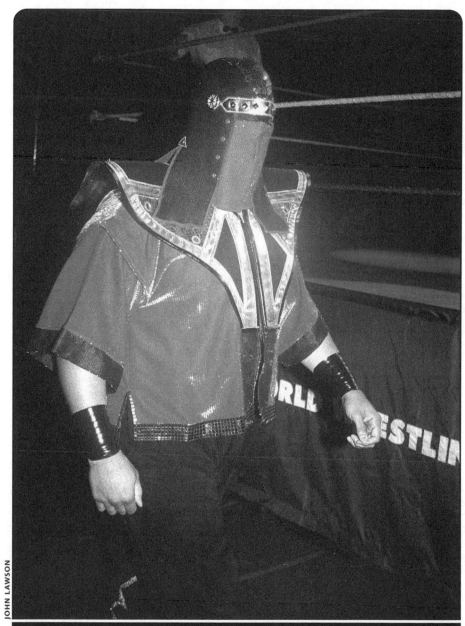

JOHN LAWSON

What's the sound of 300 pounds of crap hitting the fan? KWANG!

chanted "Shave your back!" Even in the wacky world of pro wrestling, it's not really desirable to be known as a human Chia Pet.

The third party of this gang war was the Nation of Domination, a militant black group led by Ron Simmons, whose claim to fame was being the first black world champion for WCW in the early '90s. Although everyone knew exactly who he was, the WWF decided, for some reason, to dress him up as a Roman gladiator with a powder-blue Nerf foam helmet. Rounding out the group was 400-pound power lifter Mark Henry, who had competed in the Olympic games; D-Lo Brown, who would reprise the racist gimmick prior to being let go by the WWF in 2003; and a young Rocky Maivia, who had just turned heel.

Maivia, whose real name was Duane Johnson, entered the WWF as the Blue Chipper. He was hyped as a can't-miss prospect by announcers, and a heck of a nice guy to boot. "You can't smile enough," were his instructions from the booking team. The fans hated the guy. Chants of "Rocky sucks!" and signs reading "Die Rocky Die" began to appear at arenas. Crowds absolutely despised him for two reasons. First, he was so green, or inexperienced, that he commonly botched even the simplest of moves; and second, the fans knew this guy was a complete phony. There was no way anyone would be that nice, especially in this day of antiheroes such as Steve Austin.

After seeing this approach fail miserably, the promotion took him off the road for several months and brought him back as the Rock, an arrogant asshole who always referred to himself in the third person. Now, this fans could totally believe. He eventually went on to headline every major and minor event the WWF had and to star in such major motion pictures as *The Mummy Returns* and *The Scorpion King*.

Even the elevation of the Rock, however, didn't change the course of the Gang Warz. The three coalitions fought for months, to the delight of absolutely no one. Fans didn't care, because of the 12 men involved, only two (Simmons and Rock) were charismatic or athletic enough to put on a decent bout. And the story line was simply that the three gangs didn't like each other, so obviously the WWF was banking on fans taking their natural prejudices and cheering for the white guys to beat up the blacks and the Latinos.

At least the Gang Warz was only scripted violence. The WWF also tried to create new stars in a most bizarre manner in 1999, when they started a legitimate toughman contest. The tournament, called *Brawl for All*, saw WWF superstars compete in a weird mishmash of boxing and wrestling. And as hard as it may be to believe, the matches were not scripted. Wrestlers were told to enter the ring and beat the hell out of each other. The idea was to show just how tough WWF superstars were, and to see who was legitimately the baddest apple of the bunch. Not that any of this made sense to fans at home. So this was real, and everything else was fake?

In the back of their minds, even though this was a legitimate tournament, the WWF knew who the winner would be: "Dr. Death" Steve Williams. By plowing through the tournament, Williams would be able to lay claim to being a legit badass and challenge Austin to a series of matches. Great idea in theory, but Williams was actually KO'ed in the early rounds and injured to the point that he was out for several months. The winner of the tournament, a midcarder by the name of Bart Gunn, was given the opportunity to showcase just how tough wrestlers were by taking on heavyweight boxer Eric "Butterbean" Esch at *Wrestlemania XV*. He was knocked out in 35 seconds. Oops!

With this realistic approach not yielding the best results, things were swung in the complete opposite direction, with story lines so campy and over the top that they were laughable.

The Legion of Doom, which had been absent from wrestling rings following the Rocco deal in the early 1990s, had resurfaced in the WWF as the decade was drawing to a close. In an effort to freshen the team up, Hawk and Animal were given a new teammate, Puke, portrayed by Darren Drozdov. The idea was that Droz could regurgitate upon command, and Vince McMahon thought this would somehow make for great television.

Here comes Animal of the Legion of Doom. If you look closely to the left, you can see his partner, Hawk, who has fallen down drunk. Hawk would later attempt to commit suicide by jumping off the WWF video wall. The WWF: good old-fashioned family fun!

In the story lines, Hawk became suspicious of Puke taking his place as the leader of the group. Hawk turned to drugs, which he later claimed had been given to him by Droz, to soothe the pain. During LOD matches in which he was not featured, Hawk would stumble down to ringside to do commentary (or, as he called it, "dysentery"), slurring his words, and generally making an ass of himself. Finally, Hawk could take no more, and so he climbed the large video wall where the wrestlers came out and threatened to jump.

Everyone, from the announcers to the wrestlers, "broke character" in an attempt to convince fans that what they were seeing was real. Droz climbed the wall to save Hawk, who would have nothing to do with him. Droz reached out to grab Hawk, but he accidentally on purpose pushed him over the edge.

Problem: There was about a three-second delay from when Hawk was pushed over until the guys behind the screen pushed something that more closely resembled a broom than a person over the edge of the video tower. Fans were supposed to believe that this was Hawk. It all looked incredibly fake. Which is probably just as well, since the WWF more or less blew off the angle immediately thereafter.

At least Hawk lived. Another angle saw hated policeman-turned-wrestler Big Bossman attempting to wrest the WWF title from the 500-pound Big Show (who had performed in WCW as the Giant) by mocking his dying father. Thankfully, the WWF was thoughtful enough to not claim Show was Andre the Giant's son, which is really the only kind thing that can be said about this entire angle.

The story line had Show's father dying of cancer. Bossman, humanitarian that he was, came out on stage and recited the following poem to help ease Show's pain:

> With deepest regrets and tears that are soaked,
> I'm sorry to hear your dad finally croaked.
> He lived a full life on his own terms,
> Soon he'll be buried and eaten by worms.
> But if I could have a son as stupid as you,
> I'd have wished for cancer so I would die too.
> So be brave, and be strong, get your life back on track,
> 'Cause the old bastard's dead and he ain't never comin' back!

Oddly, Show didn't take kindly to these words of comfort and in fact threatened to dismember the Bossman. Bossman didn't care. He was getting under the champ's skin. Therefore, he hunted down Big Show's mama, who brought forth another shocking revelation: Big Show was an illegitimate child. He was, in her own words, "nothing more than a bastard!"

The worst was yet to come, as WWF cameras took fans to Daddy Show's funeral. Show was delivering some kind words about his father, when what to his wondering eyes should appear? An old police car, complete with an oversized loudspeaker attached to the top. Inside was the Bossman, who had apparently stolen the car from the Blues Brothers. His voice was booming through the graveyard: "Your daddy ain't nuthin', he never was nuthin', and I'm glad the old bastard's dead!" He proceeded to run the Show over with the car. With family members distracted as they attended to Show, Bossman attached a chain to the casket and began to drive away with the casket dragging along behind the car. Show got up and, with his last ounce of strength, jumped atop the casket, riding it like a sled. Show eventually fell off, and Bossman got away with the cadaver.

The payoff to all this buildup? A championship match that lasted 90 seconds.

It wasn't the only heinous crime the Bossman perpetrated.

Al Snow was a journeyman wrestler who had achieved a level of fame on the independent circuit by carrying a mannequin head to the ring. Snow's cries of, "What does everybody want?" would be answered by the crowd: "Head!" The idea was that Snow was a guy on the verge of insanity, just one step away from a trip to the funny farm. He was, therefore, an ideal candidate for the WWF's Hardcore division, in which wrestlers bashed each other over the head with weapons such as chairs and cookie sheets.

After having his head stolen, Snow took to bringing a one-eyed stuffed deer head named Pierre to the ring. That was stolen, too. Finally, Snow began carting a live Chihuahua named Pepper to the matches.

You know what happens next. Bossman steals the dog. Bossman invites Snow to dinner. Bossman informs Snow he is actually eating Pepper. We've all seen it a thousand times.

Obviously, Pepper needed to be avenged, so Snow challenged Bossman to a Kennel from Hell match, which had never been done before (or since, thankfully). One ring, surrounded by a cage, with rabid dogs inside another cage surrounding the first. The only problem was that the dogs were more playful than rabid. Two of the dogs began humping on screen. Another simply took a dump. Snow escaped the cage as the dogs played fetch with the Bossman.

It wasn't the only time during this period that the WWF used canines for a bout. Davey Boy Smith and Val Venis took on Mankind and the Rock in a Poo Poo match, the goal of which was to throw your opponent onto a big platter of dog crap. How could those snoots in Greenwich possibly say wrestling is a lowbrow entertainment?

All of these angles and story lines, stupid as they may have been, were generally not the focal point of the promotion. There was one memorable angle, however, that encompassed the entire WWF for weeks. The Undertaker had been one of the few men who had stayed with the WWF through thick and thin. Despite idiotic angles such as his resurrection and the Underfaker, he never threatened to leave the company, remaining one of the few draws they had left. McMahon appreciated Taker's loyalty, and made sure to reward him with main events and featured story lines.

During the early days of Steve Austin's rise to glory, Undertaker's character underwent a modification. He was no longer an undead zombie, but rather a devil-worshipping freak. He recruited an unholy band, the Ministry, whose sole purpose, it seemed, was to conduct all sorts of bizarre rituals. Upon their initiation into the clan, the Undertaker would slice his new recruits' chests open and drink some of their blood.

Yep, this definitely wasn't your father's WWF.

The Ministry had one target they coveted more than any other: "Stone Cold" Steve Austin. Like any good group of Satanists, they weren't after just a championship, but rather the man's very soul. Upon his capture, Undertaker, speaking in tongues, attempted to bury Austin alive. That didn't work, so they set out to embalm him. No dice. Finally, they strapped Austin to a cross and hung him high in the air.

Oh, oh, wait. That wasn't a cross. It was a "symbol." Or so said the WWF when they were called on this little stunt. It wasn't a cross at all, and they weren't portraying a crucifixion. No way, no how. Sure, it looked just like a cross and Austin's hands and feet were bound to it just like Jesus, but it wasn't a cross, no sirree. It was a symbol.

Perhaps even more than dog poop or crucifixions, though, the so-called Attitude era of the WWF in the late '90s was categorized by an insane level of sex the likes of which wrestling had never seen before. Women began appearing out of the woodwork. Long gone were grotesque women grapplers such as Bertha Faye. In their place were hot tamales with million-dollar bodies who weren't afraid to bare it all — or at least as much as the censors would allow.

While the women in the promotion such as Rena "Sable" Mero and Tammy "Sunny" Sytch were easy on the eyes, other sexual spectacles were not. The WWF, no doubt proclaiming to believe in equal rights, decided that they needed to have something to appeal to the ladies in the crowd as well.

Enter Val Venis, former porn star (in the story lines, at least). Val made his debut in a series of vignettes in which he would be laying pipe, so to speak, with attractive females. His entrance video was classic. In between

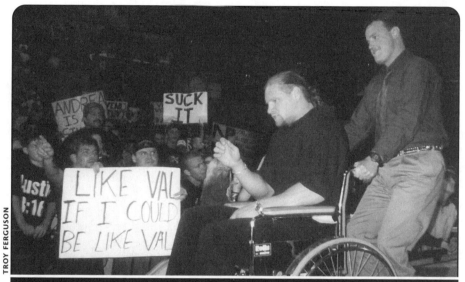

TROY FERGUSON

Val Venis with the only man who could comfort him after getting his own pee pee choppy choppied, John Wayne Bobbitt. Makes you wonder why that guy in the crowd wants to be like Val.

clips of him wiggling his hips in the ring, there were shots of foot-long hot dogs, flowers blooming, oil derricks bursting, and other blatant phallus imagery. It was all played so ridiculously over the top that most fans had a good laugh at the whole affair.

Val's feuds generally centered on his unquenchable libido. He would make off with another wrestler's wife, then show one of his "new movies" —featuring himself in bed with the guy's wife—to his rival. The rival would get upset, and they would have a match. Simple enough.

But then Val began feuding with the Japanese group known as Kaintei, led by Wally Yamaguchi. Yamaguchi would often bring his "wife" with him to the ring, a young Oriental girl who looked to be about 15 years old. What's a former porn star to do? Bag the enemy's wife, of course! Venis debuted his latest movie, entitled *Land of the Rising Venis*. Yamaguchi was furious. He vowed the ultimate revenge: he would cut off Val's wiener. To show he meant business, Yamaguchi brought a large sausage out on stage and proceeded to chop it in half with a samurai sword. He also issued his now-infamous battle cry: "I choppy choppy your pee pee!"

Sure enough, the following week the evil Japanese cartel abducted Val and hauled him backstage. Stripped naked, with his hands tied together, our heroic porn star seemed to have no means of escape. However, just as Wally lifted his sword, the lights suddenly went out. Screams were heard.

The following week, Val was pushed out to the ring in a wheelchair by John Wayne Bobbitt. Bobbitt, you will recall, had gained notoriety by having his own member lopped off by his wife in 1993. If there was anyone who could console Val, surely it was him. Instead, Val hopped out of the wheelchair, swiveled his hips, and claimed that thanks to shrinkage, the Big Valbowski was still intact. Would-be groupies in the crowd cheered.

There were other men who were in charge of satisfying the ladies as well. A second-generation star by the name of Shawn Stasiak was given the persona of a sex slave. He was managed by three women, the Pretty Mean Sisters (PMS), who used Stasiak for his body. He was, according to PMS, nothing more than a piece of meat, so they named him just that: Meat. The trio would browbeat their boy, "forcing" him to have sex. He would traipse down to the ring in his tights, which were fashioned to look like a pair of underwear, and do their bidding. On occasion, they would simply tease Meat, and he would wrestle with an erection poking his opponent. Strangely, some superstars didn't like to wrestle Meat, neither the man nor the anatomy.

Another oddball sex star was created in the form of Harry "Beaver" Cleavage, a spoof of the classic TV show *Leave It to Beaver*. He was introduced to fans via a series of black-and-white vignettes that appeared to take place in a home straight out of the 1950s. Harry, wearing a beanie and a bow tie, would look to his "mother," a scantily dressed honey pie in her early twenties. For example, during one skit, Harry spilled milk in his lap. As his mother cleaned it up (and appeared for all the world to be giving the guy a hand job), she stated, "That's better—now we have a dry, clean Harry Beaver. No one likes a sloppy beaver!" Canned laughter followed.

The character was eventually dumped and it was explained that Harry and his "mom" were actually a real-life couple. This led to a domestic violence angle, in which the former Beaver beat his wife. It was almost enough to make one long for the dim-witted comedy that the 1950s skits provided.

While there were men for the women to ogle at, the WWF realized that their target audience wanted to see hot chicks, preferably scantily dressed ones. The company did their best to oblige, carting out one surgically enhanced bimbo after another as commentator Jerry Lawler squealed in delight at the "puppies" (WWF slang for breasts) on display. On several occasions, the puppies would get loose, as the women accidentally on purpose flashed the crowd.

One of the first women the WWF introduced as a "diva" was a blond bombshell from Fort Monmouth, New Jersey, by the name of Tammy Sytch. She had gained experience in the Smoky Mountain region, and had caught the eye of Vince McMahon, who believed she could be a superstar. He christened her Sunny, and she was an instant sensation with the men in the crowd.

Her boyfriend was Chris Candido, who had entered the company as Bodydonna Skip, an image-obsessed physical trainer. He was quickly joined by Zip (Tom Prichard), and Sunny managed the pair to the WWF tag team titles. However, after the team lost the belts, she turned against them and joined whoever had the straps at the time. The Bodydonnas fought back by introducing Cloudy, a guy dressed up like Sunny. It was as funny as it sounds. Which is to say, not funny at all. In fact, Candido was so upset with the angle that he quit the promotion several weeks later.

It wasn't the last cross-dresser the WWF would pawn off on fans. Mark Henry had dropped his Olympic strongman character in exchange for something radically different. He became Sexual Chocolate, ladies man extraordinaire. He had been making passes at Chyna, a former square-jawed, muscle-bound behildebeast, who, through the miracle of about 20 different plastic surgeries, went on to pose nude for *Playboy* in one of their best-selling issues ever. Whether this was due to men wanting to see her naked or just curious about whether she actually had a penis, no one knows for sure. She did, however, inform her fans that it was through her hard work that she made it into *Playboy*, a statement she made in a speech on WWF TV in which she spoke of the photo spread as an honor that rivaled winning the Nobel Prize. Oddly, she did not thank her plastic surgeon. Hmmm.

Anyway, after several weeks of intense wooing, it appeared as though Henry had won over the not-so-fair maiden. She asked him how he'd feel about having a threesome with her girlfriend Sammy. Well, hell, they didn't call him Sexual Chocolate for nothing! Bring it on!

Chyna introduced Mark to Sammy, and the two began to mash, fondling each other's naughty bits. As Mark reached down to get him a little somethin' somethin', he suddenly jumped back and shrieked in terror, "Oh, sweet Jesus! You've got a penis!" The skank pulled off her wig, replying,

"Why do you think they call me Sammy, baby?" Mark retreated to the bathroom, where he vomited, an action no doubt repeated by millions watching at home.

It wouldn't be the last time the poor guy was humiliated on national TV. Some have even speculated that Vince McMahon was trying to drive the guy out of the company because he had shown so little ability in the ring. However, McMahon had signed him to an unheard-of ten-year contract and therefore couldn't simply fire him. Henry would have to quit to get McMahon out of the big-money deal. It didn't work, as Henry viewed it all as "just an act" and did whatever McMahon asked. Good for you, dude. Stick it to the man.

Since Sexual Chocolate's erotic desires were getting him into trouble, he was advised to undergo therapy to get things under control. This led to a haha-larious series of skits in which he explained to a therapist that he'd lost his virginity at age seven and had also slept with his sister. When queried about the last time he had done this, he stated, "About a week ago." The therapist, rather than being repulsed, hopped out of her chair and gave him a lap dance. Well, why wouldn't she?

Desperate to find a woman who could keep up with his libido, Henry recruited a most unusual candidate: 75-year-old Mae Young. Mae began to show up on WWF TV with the Fabulous Moolah, an elderly woman wrestler who had the distinction of holding the WWF women's title for twenty-odd years, starting in the late 1960s. Mae was portrayed as an out-of-control grandmother who drank, smoked, and played poker. Strip poker.

She planned to show off her goods at *Royal Rumble 2000*, which featured a swimsuit competition. All the usual suspects were there, displaying their wares to a packed arena and to hundreds of thousands more fans on pay-per-view. Suddenly, from the back, Mae came staggering out, claiming that her fans wanted to see *her* puppies. Sure enough, she took off her top, displaying her withered funbags to the crowd. Even the lascivious Lawler was repulsed, stating, "Those aren't puppies—Those are Sharpeis!"

With such a pedigree, it should come as no shock that she hooked up with Henry. Not only did they do the wild thing, but Henry also impregnated her. Of course, had anyone actually thought about it, they would have realized that a 75-year-old woman couldn't have a baby. Mae herself even confirmed that it wasn't possible when she let the world know that the last time she'd had a period was in 1957.

As if the thought of a leathery old woman being on the rag wasn't enough to turn wrestling fans celibate, the WWF decided it would be fun to let everyone see the actual birth. Was it a boy? Was it a girl? No, silly. It was a hand. Rumor has it that McMahon wanted her to give birth to a douche bag, but that the network nixed that idea. So fans got a slime-covered rubber hand instead.

Amazingly, fans tuned in to *Raw* in record numbers to see just what insane stunt they would try next. By using shock TV as a magnet, the Federation was able to lure people into watching the wrestling action, which, thanks to Foley, Austin, and Rock, was usually tremendous. Folks who had never been wrestling fans before now regularly reserved Monday nights to get their fix.

Just as the WWF was about to conquer the world, however, they were rocked with a major defection. It wasn't a wrestler, but rather their head writer. One of the men who had pioneered the WWF's Attitude era was leaving the company and heading to the competition.

WCW was about to get injected with a dose of Attitude.

A lethal dose.

Vince Russo Presents: How to Lose $60 Million in Just 12 Months!

October 11, 1999 was supposed to be the turning point for WCW, the last day that the promotion would wallow in low ratings and even lower buy rates. It was all going to change from this date forward, and it would all be due to the hiring of one man: Vince Russo, a man who had never even been inside a wrestling ring.

Depending on whom you believe, Russo is either one of the greatest geniuses or the most blatant con men the wrestling world has ever known. He was a behind-the-scenes writer for the WWF who, by his own admission if no one else's, had turned that sinking ship around in the late '90s. He came up with a new style of programming, "crash TV," that combined equal amounts of sex, action, and shocking story line twists. Since he had "saved the WWF," it was assumed that he could duplicate his success with another promotion. He certainly convinced the higher-ups at Turner headquarters of this, flying into Atlanta on a Friday in September 1999 and leaving with a signed contract just two days later.

His first show in the promotion was actually a success. Thanks to an incredible amount of self-promotion, fans were curious to see just who this Vince Russo was and what he could do with WCW. Going into the first show, however, he promised that he would never be seen on camera, appearing off camera instead as one-half of a mysterious duo known as the Powers That Be. This buzz, combined with an interesting story line throughout the show, netted *Nitro* its best rating in six weeks. *Raw* still murdered them in the ratings, but it was definitely a step in the right direction.

Russo promised that big changes were in store for the company, the first of which was a drastic alteration in the structure of story lines and matches within the promotion. Russo believed that for a wrestling promotion to succeed, it needed to emphasize entertainment, such as skits and interviews, over in-ring action. More than anything, however, he believed that they needed sex, sex, and more sex.

Tits-and-ass was the name of Russo's game. Countless women were brought into the promotion for no reason other than to provide eye candy to those in attendance. Strippers accompanied nearly every wrestler to the ring and would often compete in mud matches, gravy matches, and any other type of contest Russo could come up with. The point wasn't athletic competition, but rather to display their barely concealed flesh to audiences at home. It didn't matter that these women couldn't wrestle, nor that their acting ability rated somewhere between that of a porn star and a *Jerry Springer* guest. What mattered was that, in Russo's mind, at least, sex sold.

It wasn't just breasty bimbos, either. Entire story lines were centered on sex. An angle was created in which hated heel Shane Douglas stole Billy Kidman's girlfriend, Torrie Wilson. Skits were shown of the two new lovers mocking Kidman as they lounged in hotel beds together. One week, however, the cameras didn't stop rolling, and it was revealed that Douglas couldn't "rise to the occasion." Hilarity ensued, setting up wrestling's first-ever "Viagra on a Pole" match. Douglas won the bout, and was henceforth able to pop a boner at will.

While the sex invasion was one of the most notable modifications to *Nitro*, something slightly less noticeable also began to take shape. Hardcore wrestling fans had long preferred *Nitro* over *Raw*, thanks to the high-flying cruiserweight action the company provided. Even during the heyday of the nWo, when the focus was on Nash, Hogan, and little else, plenty of time was allotted to the cruiserweight division, which provided wrestling fans with the fast-paced, athletic style of wrestling they loved.

Russo changed that. He didn't feel that the smaller men, primarily the Mexicans and Japanese whom Eric Bischoff had imported years earlier, could connect with the American wrestling fan. He stated such in an interview with Dave Richards on the now defunct Wrestleline.com: "You will never ever, ever, ever, ever see the Japanese wrestler or the Mexican wrestler over in American mainstream wrestling. And the simple reason for that is, even myself, I'm an American, and I don't want to sound like a big bigot or a racist or anything like that, but I'm an American . . . if I'm watching wrestling here in America, I don't give a shit about a Japanese guy. I don't give a shit about a Mexican guy. I'm from America, and that's what I want to see."

This being Russo's thinking, it's obvious why talented grapplers such as many of the Mexican *luchadores* who had thrilled fans in previous years were given insulting bit parts. Chavo Guerrero became an Amway salesman, for example, and later rode around on a stick pony while wearing a sombrero. Juventud Guerrera, another star of the division, resorted to hitting people over the head with a tequila bottle. And just to belabor the point, Russo once had all the Mexicans fight in a battle royal. That in itself wouldn't have been bad, but when you consider that they were fighting over a piñata, it becomes a bit questionable.

Although American cruiserweights were promoted, they were given such ridiculous gimmicks that they had no chance of getting over. Prince

Iaukea, who had long been a jobber in the midcard, suddenly transformed into The Artist Formerly Known as Prince Iaukea, complete with purple lighting and a valet named Paisley. While it could be argued that this was at least somewhat clever, it was a one-note joke that was presented week after week to fans who simply didn't care about the guy. Having him dress up like an eccentric pop singer didn't change that fact.

The death of the cruiserweight division, though, had perhaps more to do with Russo's petty attempts to get even with his former employer. When Russo had moved to WCW, he'd brought along fellow writer Ed Ferrara. Since the two now had their own stage, they often used it to grind axes with their former bosses in the WWF. And there was no one they disliked more than the WWF's director of talent relations, Jim Ross.

To fans watching at home, Jim Ross was "Good Ol' J.R.," a television announcer. He wore a cowboy hat and spoke with a southern twang, always rooting for the good guys and crying foul at any move a rule breaker made. That was Jim Ross to the general public. Behind the scenes, Ross was a powerful player for the WWF. He handled contracts and had a lot of say in who did and didn't get a push within the company. Likely due to the fact that Ross preferred in-ring action to over-the-top gimmickry, Russo and Ferrara often butted heads with the man.

Now that they had their own show, they were going to give Ross hell. Ferrara became an on-screen character called Oklahoma, named after Ross's home state. He wore a little cowboy hat and spouted off with commentary that mocked J.R.'s. His foreign object of choice was a bottle of BBQ sauce, something Ross was in the process of marketing. In a show of incredibly poor taste, Oklahoma even knocked Ross for having Bell's palsy, a disease that had left half his face paralyzed.

All this would have been annoying enough, but soon he began to wrestle. Despite the fact that he tipped the scales at around 260 pounds, he somehow became the cruiserweight champion (weight limit 225) by beating Madusa. And before you ask, yes, Madusa was a woman that just so happened to be in a men's division. Got a headache yet?

This sort of thing happened all the time. It didn't matter that fans actually liked Ross, what mattered was that Russo and Ferrara viewed this as their chance to get even. And it didn't matter that fans didn't get what was going on, at least not to Russo. What mattered was that he, Vince Russo, was turning WCW into his own personal WWF.

And make no mistake about it—Russo desperately wanted WCW to become the WWF. So much so that he blatantly copied ideas from the company and presented them as WCW's own. Granted, they may have been Russo's ideas to begin with, but that doesn't change the fact that fans had already seen them and associated them with the WWF. Therefore, while they may have been from Russo's brain initially, no one knew who Russo was until he arrived in WCW. They did, however, know the WWF's characters.

For example, fans knew who the WWF's Road Dogg was, as he was one of the Federation's most popular performers. What fans didn't know was that Road Dogg was actually a guy by the name of Brian Armstrong, and that his brother Brad wrestled for WCW. Without this knowledge, fans had no clue why Brad Armstrong, under the guise of Buzzkill, was suddenly dressing and acting just like Road Dogg.

While Brad was far and away a better in-ring performer than his brother was, he suffered from a decided lack of charisma. Brad's other brothers had also found their way into the business, mainly on independent shows throughout the southern United States. None had been able match the success their father, "Bullet Bob" Armstrong, had achieved during the 1960s and '70s in Tennessee. In fact, of all the brothers, only one had ever "made it," and that was Brian, who was often viewed as the least technically sound of the brothers inside the ring. Quite honestly, Brian appeared to have the bleakest future in the business due to what was perceived as a very unmarketable look.

Vince McMahon had other ideas. He brought Armstrong to the WWF as Jeff Jarrett's roadie, at a time when Jarrett was attempting to take over Nashville by way of the World Wrestling Federation. How, exactly, being a wrestling champion was supposed to garner him a singing contract is anyone's guess, but the character was pushed for years using that very logic.

After Jarrett bolted the promotion, Vince tweaked the gimmick and allowed Armstrong to speak. Voilà: the "Road Dogg" was born. He paired up with "Badd Ass" Billy Gunn to form the New Age Outlaws. They joined up with D-Generation X and became one of the most popular teams in the history of the WWF. While Brian didn't have Brad's in-ring ability, he did have charisma, something that Brad lacked. Russo, however, felt that he could re-create the Road Dogg's popularity by using Brad in his brother's place in WCW, and he set out to copy Road Dogg in every conceivable way. Same intro music, same opening spiel on the microphone, same basic look.

The Buzzkill character immediately showed fans that the WCW creative department had all the imagination of a Xerox machine. It made WCW look second-rate, because they were not coming up with their own ideas, but rather copying gimmicks and characters made famous in the WWF, and poorly at that. The music kinda sounded the same . . . the character sort of looked the same . . . but it wasn't the same. It was as if WCW were doing a tribute show to the WWF. As was often the case, Russo had come up with the idea quickly and wanted to get it on TV immediately, not giving Brad time to perfect the character. In fact, Russo had him on TV so quickly that Brad was unable to grow out his hair, and he was forced to use braids in an attempt to duplicate his brother's look.

Wrestlers who weren't asked to directly rip off the WWF were no more fortunate. Consider the sad case of Mike Awesome. Awesome had made a name for himself as a dominant ECW world champion, and he was looking to shock the industry by jumping to WCW while still holding ECW's top belt. The heat the guy felt when ECW fans and management found out about this was incredible, and it could do nothing but boost his entrance into Turnerland.

Shortly after his arrival, however, Russo decided to change his gimmick entirely, from a career killer to a comedy figure trapped in the 1970s. Dubbed "That '70s Guy," Awesome would come to the ring bedecked in a leisure suit, gold chains, and feathered hair, looking as though he had just hopped off the dance floor with Tony Manero. Rather than showcasing Awesome's incredible in-ring skills, they gave him a talk show segment, "The Lava Lamp Lounge." That flopped. Of course, how could Awesome succeed when he would use horrible pickup lines on his female guests like, "Are you from Tennessee? Because you're the only 10 I see!" If you think that is a good line, you should probably move out of your parents' basement and try it out during your next social function.

Deciding, for some reason, that they really needed to punch things up, Russo went so far as to get Awesome a bus painted to look just like the one from *The Partridge Family*, a TV show about a band in the early 1970s. WCW then went to the expense of bringing in former *Diff'rent Strokes* star Gary Coleman to act as Awesome's stooge. If only they'd got Todd Bridges out of jail and resurrected Dana Plato, they might have been on to something.

As was often the case, after all the buildup Russo decided to drop the character in favor of his next grand scheme, which no doubt caused Awesome to breathe a sigh of relief. That comfort was short-lived, however, as Awesome was subsequently turned into the "Fat Chick Thriller," and his whole persona was built around being attracted to (and therefore saving) obese women in the audience. It almost seemed like they were giving Awesome terrible characters on purpose, hoping he would quit so they could get out of paying his contractual dues. To Awesome's credit, he stuck it out, forcing WCW to pay him every last penny they'd promised.

Bill Demott didn't have it much better. A huge man who was amazingly agile, he was given horrible character after horrible character to portray during his WCW stint. Finally, he had accepted life as "The Laughing Man, Hugh Morris." His gimmick was that he laughed. Then he would frown. Then he'd start laughing again. Was this a good gimmick? No, of course not. But it was far better than what Russo had in store for him.

Russo's idea was to build a stable of wrestlers wrapped in the American flag and call them MIA — Misfits in Action. Russo took a handful of workers who had been floundering in the midcard and gave them a bimbo named Major Gunns (played by fitness model Tylene Buck) as a focal point. See, she was Major Gunns because she had large boobies. You can't buy subtlety like that.

Hugh was the group's leader, and was flanked by other military men such as Corporal Cajun and Major Stash. A funny aside about Stash: he was originally to be dubbed Private Stash, and the gimmick was that he smoked a lot of weed, which he would hide. Get it? Private Stash? Well, the guy who played Stash (and who had formerly bombed as "Heavy Metal" Van Hammer) was upset at being "only" a private, so Russo relented and changed him to major. Only in professional wrestling.

Being that everyone had military names, it was decided that "Hugh Morris" didn't really fit. Demott therefore went before a live crowd, and the announcers proclaimed that he was "shooting," or breaking script and telling the truth. It turned out, according to Hugh, that his last name wasn't really Morris. Thousands of fans in the arena and millions watching at home were no doubt shocked and/or appalled by this revelation, if sitting on your hands in silence with a bored look indicates being shocked and/or appalled. Hugh dropped the bomb that his last name was actually "Rection," and his middle initial was "G." That's right, his name was Hugh G. Rection. Russo was no doubt pleased—he finally got to name a wrestler after a penis.

The MIA angle not only nearly killed off Demott, but Booker Huffman as well. Huffman, known to fans the world over as Booker T, was known for many years as one-half of the tag team known as Harlem Heat. Well, actually, for many years, Booker T was simply known as the *good* half of Harlem Heat, carrying brother Stevie Ray to decent matches against all comers. He had come so far from the initial gimmick WCW had given him, which was arguably the most racist gimmick of all time. You see, the original incarnation of Harlem Heat portrayed the brothers as slaves.

Yes, slaves, like Kunte Kinte in *Roots*. The two were even bound together with shackles and chains. Apparently, the memo stating that this kind of thing had been abolished 130 years prior never made it to the WCW creative team. They were led to the ring by a rich southerner (Colonel Robert Parker). One-half of the duo was actually known as Kole. See, because he was black. Like coal. Get it? Thankfully, although this original idea was presented at a few nontelevised events, crowd reaction was so violent that it never made it to air. Still, that a promotion would even ponder doing something like that less than 15 years ago should give you a good idea just how far behind the times wrestling can be.

Booker had not only overcome that horrific first gimmick, but he was also able to move up the ranks and dominate the WCW tag scene for years. Finally, he caught a break when his brother injured himself, giving him his first real shot as a singles competitor. And he truly did excel, with a memorable series of matches against Chris Benoit that were among the best things that WCW did in the late '90s. He had an incredible mix of skills; he was great in the ring, good on the microphone, and knew how to work a crowd. Even those in the back loved him, because he did whatever he was told without question. In fact, it seemed that everything was pointing toward an eventual world title run for Booker.

Leave it to Russo to throw that out the window and repackage Booker with a lame-ass army gimmick and throw him in with the Misfits. Despite months of buildup as a breakout superstar, Booker inexplicably became G.I. Bro, which had been the first persona he had upon breaking into the business. Booker did as asked, of course, donning the army fatigues and thus destroying any momentum he'd previously had.

Even the nitwits running WCW at the time could see that this angle was going nowhere, and, shockingly, they did the right thing and scrapped it entirely. Booker T went back to being his old roof-raising self, and he finally snared that world title that many felt should have been his years earlier. Perhaps it was Russo's way of paying Booker back for the G.I. Bro gimmick, but there are some who claim he was given the belt solely due to the fact that it would hurt a racial discrimination lawsuit filed by several former WCW workers.

And that was a huge problem for Russo. Not that particular lawsuit, mind you, but rather the fact that in his quest for ratings, he was stepping over the lines of what TNT considered acceptable. Sure, he had bumped ratings up slightly . . . but at what cost? He had created countless head-aches for the suits at Turner with his outrageous programming.

As a retort of sorts, he created characters based on those within the company whom he felt were stunting WCW's growth. Remember Disciples of Apocalypse, the motorcycle gang featuring the guy with the misplaced nipple from the WWF? They were put into three-piece suits as a tag team known as Creative Control, an inside jab at the folks who oversaw (and often censored) WCW programming. They were even given a rather size-able push, not due to any talent they had, but rather to get the goat of Turner personnel.

There was also a similar tag team portrayed by Lodi and Lenny Lane. Their original gimmick saw them as quasi-homosexuals known as the West Hollywood Blondes. The pair would come out sucking matching lollipops and making eyes at each other. Turner executives didn't care for this and nixed the gimmick. When Russo arrived, he brought Lenny and Lodi back, this time as brothers, and teamed them up with Stacy Keibler in a group known as Standards & Practices. Again, this was more to irritate those within the Turner organization than to entice fans to come out to the matches.

These ideas may have been entertaining to Russo, but others within the Turner empire were not amused. Backstage, things were starting to boil over, because even with Russo's outlandish changes, ratings weren't rising as quickly as expected. And even though ratings were up a bit, pay-per-view buy rates and house-show attendance, which were where the company made the bulk of its money, were way down. This led to heated debates about the direction of the company.

The capper was a showdown between Russo and his immediate supe-riors in the organization, Brad Siegel and Bill Busch, over who the WCW

World Champion should be. Russo pushed for Tank Abbott, a shoot fighter who had never done a thing in pro wrestling and looked like an out-of-work bum. Now, make no mistake; Tank Abbott was a legitimate badass who could beat the hell out of almost anyone walking the planet. But he had never accomplished anything in the wrestling business and fans didn't take him seriously, thanks to his role as a groupie for Three Count, a boy-band tag team. Even Busch and Siegel, neither of whom had much of a background in wrestling, saw this as a horrible idea and vetoed the title change.

Russo was sent home. For the next three months the company floundered, although really no more so than it did with him in charge. Others within the company didn't like the idea of Russo being paid for doing nothing, so eventually an agreement was reached by all parties that brought Russo back into the fold. He returned in April with a most unexpected guest — Eric Bischoff, who had also been ousted from the promotion following the collapse of the nWo. The idea was that Bischoff could help oversee some of Russo's more questionable ideas and perhaps control him to some degree. WCW vacated all of its titles and ditched all of its story lines, effectively resetting the promotion in hopes of creating something fresh. And Vince Russo, who had sworn up and down that he would never appear on camera, opened the show live in the ring.

Much like the very first show of his WCW tenure, this event was very well laid out. Bischoff and Russo appeared with all of the younger talent in WCW, claiming that these men had been held back by the likes of Hogan, Flair, and the rest of the "Millionaire's Club." This allowed many new, fresh feuds to be set in motion. Again, the ratings for the week nudged up slightly due to the interest fans had in seeing just what WCW had up their sleeves.

Within weeks, however, things began to fall apart once more, mostly due to Russo's manic booking. If there's one thing Vince Russo loved to do while writing wrestling programs, it was to swerve the fans — in other words, to lead them so that they would expect one thing to happen, but then deliver something completely different. It didn't matter if it made sense or if it would eventually make money, it just had to fool people.

Think of it this way: if Russo was managing the local Pizza Hut, you'd order a pizza and they'd deliver a newspaper. Sure, it was a surprise, but it didn't make much sense, nor did you want to order from them again. But it sure fooled you, didn't it? These so-called swerves took place with such frequency that the only shocking event was when no swerve took place at all.

The most disappointing aspect of these swerves were that they killed off the remaining WCW fan base by creating events that fans simply didn't want to see. In the weeks leading up to *The Great American Bash 2000* pay-per-view, Russo promised an event that would change the entire landscape of wrestling. It was something that would be truly groundbreaking, and, best of all, there wasn't a thing that Vince McMahon could do about it. Fan expectations began to build. What could it be? Could "Stone Cold" Steve Austin be on his way to WCW? Maybe the Rock? If it was going to be this groundbreaking, this earth-shattering, it had to be something huge, right?

Well, it was shocking, and there wasn't anything that McMahon could do about it. Truthfully, though, even if McMahon had had the power to stop this event, he wouldn't have used it. For on that night, WCW turned its number-one babyface into a bad guy: yes, Goldberg became a heel. It was, again, something that the fans didn't want, but that didn't matter — what mattered was that they'd been fooled once again. And Russo seemed to take delight in that more than anything else.

The problem now was that these paying fans, the ones who wanted to see Goldberg demolish the heels in the company, were beginning to leave the promotion, this time for good. Crowds began to dwindle, and pay-per-view buy rates, which had been bad before, began to reach critical levels. And things were about to get much, much worse, as nothing Russo had ever booked or would book would do as much irreparable damage as what was about to unfold.

During WCW's hot run in 1997, Eric Bischoff brokered a deal to create a motion picture based on the promotion. Warner Brothers released the film, entitled *Ready to Rumble*, to U.S. theaters on April 7, 2000. In addition to various WCW wrestlers, the movie featured Scott Caan, Oliver Platt, Rose McGowan, and David Arquette. Here's what it says on the back of the video release:

> Q: What's more fun than a wrestling fan who drives a pump-it-and-dump-it sewage truck and sucks up the sweet air of World Championship Wrestling glory at night?
>
> A: Two wrestling fans — Gordie and Sean!

Actually, the answer to that question *should* read:

> "Anything! A trip to the dentist, getting hit in the head with a lead pipe, a Paulie Shore movie marathon . . . you name it, because this movie absolutely sucks!"

Truth in advertising aside, *Ready to Rumble* is the story of two hardcore wrestling fans, Gordie (Arquette) and Sean (Caan). The pair are just like any other marks, except for the fact that they think everything in pro wrestling is real and are really, *really* stupid. Aside from watching *Nitro*, their favorite pastime is sticking their fingers up their butts. No, really. And that's a plot point in the film, as they use their stinky fingers to get all kinds of stuff, like free Slurpies.

Gordie's father doesn't approve of his son wasting his life; he wants him to become a cop, just like every other member of the family. He also doesn't want his son wasting all his time and money on pro wrestling. Strangely, though, he never lectures him about jamming his hand up his anus.

The hero of the story is a wrestler named Jimmy King, who just so happens to be the WCW World Champion. This displeases booker/promoter/all-around bad guy Titus Sinclair, who decides to double-cross our hero with the help of Diamond Dallas Page. During a title match, Page begins to legitimately pummel King and screws him out of the belt. King is left for dead by Sinclair and leaves the arena in disgrace.

After this tragedy, Gordie and Sean head home, with tears literally filling their eyes. This blurs Gordie's vision, and the hapless pair wreck the septic truck. In an ironic twist of fate, a toilet paper truck then shows up and wrecks as well. For some bizarre, unexplained reason, Gordie and Sean view this as a sign from God above that they need to give up their chosen careers and track down King.

Gordie and Sean find a down-on-his-luck King hiding out in a trailer park, dressing in drag to avoid bill collectors. They convince King to take off the skirt and get back in the ring to fight DDP. Since he would be ejected if he even showed up at the arena, the boys hide King in a Porta-Potty, which they wheel into the backstage area. During DDP's interview, he hops out of the can, attacks Page, and pins him. Sinclair, furious at this, demands a cage match with DDP and King at the next pay-per-view.

The boys track down a crazy old shoot fighter to train King. The geezer has no time for young whippersnappers like Jimmy, and he beats him with a strategically placed kick to the 'nads. King takes his newfound shoot fighting knowledge into his triple-decker steel cage battle against Page. However, Sinclair decides to not play fair and has all the heels attack King in an attempt to put him out of wrestling for good.

Just when things look most bleak, out comes Gordie with his new *CHiPs* gimmick. He proceeds to smash the cage door open with his motorcycle. Meanwhile, high atop the cage, King gently places DDP onto the mesh, and DDP immediately falls about 37 stories before landing on the mat. What with the Owen Hart tragedy — the grappler actually fell to his death while rappelling to the ring from the rafters — this probably wasn't the most tasteful way to finish the bout. The movie ends with King holding the WCW belt high over his head, and everyone lives happily ever after, most likely with their fingers up their asses.

Upon release of the film, WCW invited Arquette to attend *Nitro* in the hope of cross-promoting the television show and the movie. With the increased exposure *Nitro* would provide (to an ideal target audience), odds were that *Ready to Rumble* would draw more people out to the theaters. And with Arquette's presence at the show, maybe *Entertainment Tonight* might do a feature on WCW. Who knows, maybe he could even convince his wife, *Friends* star Courtney Cox, to show up as well. Either way, it appeared to be a win-win situation.

During a production meeting prior to *Nitro*, commentator Tony Schiavone joked that with all this publicity they were receiving, perhaps they should even make Arquette champion. Everyone laughed. How funny would that be — a 150-pound weakling actor as champion. Har har!

But one man at the table wasn't laughing: Vince Russo. In fact, he thought that it was a great idea. He was alone in this thinking. Even Arquette, himself a lifelong wrestling fan, knew people would hate the idea, and tried to talk him out of it. Russo would have none of it, convinced that this was just the thing WCW needed.

The WCW world title was held up following a disputed ending to a title match between Jeff Jarrett and DDP on *Nitro*. The belt was then put up for grabs the next night on *Thunder* in a tag-team encounter featuring Jarrett and Bischoff against Page and Arquette. The end came when Arquette speared Bischoff, and referee Mickey Jay counted the pin fall.

Fans were outraged. Some threw garbage into the ring, while others flooded WCW offices with hate mail. No one could believe that even WCW would do something this dumb. As if it weren't bad enough having Arquette as a fluke champion, he actually began to defend the belt against legitimate contenders. Several wrestlers actually *lost* to Arquette, including Tank Abbott, the shoot fighter that Russo had wanted as champ several months earlier. These wins set up a triple-decker cage match, with Arquette defending the strap against DDP and Jarrett at the *Slamboree 2000* pay-per-view. The match went back and forth as Jarrett and Page slugged it out. Arquette hid in the corner. At the end of the match, Arquette turned against his friend Page and gave the belt to Jarrett.

It was yet another of Vince Russo's "shocking" swerves.

David Arquette's championship tenure garnered WCW the mainstream publicity they had so desired. It was covered in the next morning's *USA Today*, which Russo trumpeted as a huge success. However, a closer look at the situation reveals that the experiment was anything but a success and was, in fact, the kiss of death for the company. While ratings remained about the same as they had been before the title switch, WCW pay-per-view numbers took a massive hit. The buy rate for *Slamboree 2000*, featuring Arquette defending his title for the first time on pay-per-view, was a 0.14, one of the lowest in the history of the company.

The thing that no one understood, especially Russo, was that while the WWF was presenting all their outlandish angles and characters, they still had wrestlers on top that people cared about. Men like Mick Foley and Steve Austin connected with the fans. David Arquette did not.

Following the Arquette title run, nothing really mattered. It didn't matter that Russo turned into a complete and utter egomaniac, booking himself to be the lead heel in the promotion, booking himself to beat Ric Flair in a cage, and booking himself to win the world title. It didn't matter that characters turned on a weekly basis in nonsensical swerves. And it didn't matter that Russo did a shoot interview calling Hulk Hogan a piece of shit, nor that Hogan left the company, never to return.

None of it mattered because no one was around to see it.

Fans abandoned the company en masse. In 2000, following all of Russo's sex and swerves and inexplicable title changes, ratings dropped to less than 2.5. Average house-show attendance in October 1999 was around 4,500 fans. In 2000, that number dropped to less than 1,800. And *Starrcade*, WCW's biggest show of the year, drew a measly 0.11, or 5 percent of what they had done for *Starrcade 1997*.

Amazingly, they had lost 95 percent of their pay-per-view audience in just three years.

Ninety-five per cent of their paying audience gone, never to return.

The end result? In 2000, with Vince Russo as the lead booker for the majority of the year, WCW lost over $60 million.

In December of 2000, Russo was sent home once again, this time for good. The company hobbled along until March, when Turner execs canceled both *Nitro* and *Thunder* and put the business up for sale.

It is unfair to blame the death of WCW entirely on one man, although a case can certainly be made for that. In reality, the company had been dying since the heyday of the nWo, which was that one brief period in which the stars aligned and all was right in WCW's world. Truthfully, though, from the Black Scorpion to the minimovies of the early '90s to the 20 different versions of the nWo, WCW was always a promotion just one or two steps away from disaster.

It just so happened that Vince Russo was the cancer for which there was no cure.

The Less Things Change, The More They Stay the Same

It had taken years, long, hard years, but Vince McMahon had finally done it. They said it couldn't be done, but he knew it could be. He *knew* it could be. And he knew he was just the man to do it. It had come to pass: the World Wrestling Federation had driven World Championship Wrestling out of business. Finally, he had what he always wanted.

Vince McMahon was the proud owner of a brand-new pro wrestling monopoly.

The man everyone from the U.S. government to Ted Turner to the FCC had tried to destroy had triumphed. He had beat them all. Not only that, but now he, Vince McMahon, was a billionaire too. That's how good WWF business had been the past two years. It had been so good, in fact, that he was able to wipe out the company that had been a thorn in his side for the past 20 years.

McMahon couldn't help but revel in the situation. Just five years earlier, WCW was clobbering the WWF in the ratings and making hundreds of millions of dollars a year doing it. In 2001, McMahon purchased WCW for around $4 million. Four measly million. That wasn't even pocket change to McMahon.

That wasn't the last of the good news, either. The renegade promotion known as Extreme Championship Wrestling was gone too. In fact, Paul Heyman, the owner of the company, had come to McMahon begging for work. The promotion that often mocked the WWF and its superstars had not only gone under, it had gone under and given itself to McMahon. That was sweet as well.

Still, McMahon needed this. He needed all this good news, the opportunities that owning his competition would allow. For while he was a genius inside the wrestling business, he was becoming a laughingstock outside it.

With much bravado, McMahon had commissioned the building of a wild football league known as the XFL. This was to be McMahon's breakout success, in which he duplicated his WWF formula for a much larger audience: National Football League fans. He did this initially by claiming that NFL players were nothing more than a bunch of "pantywaists," which probably did little to endear him to his target audience. His approach was to draw folks to the game in another way, which he explained in an interview with *Playboy* in their February 2001 issue. After comparing riding his motorcycle to having a 12-foot penis, he explained the concept behind the XFL:

> There will be controversy. If there isn't, we will create it. The real show is on the sidelines, in the stands, in the locker rooms, and we're going to show it all. Not the lily-white, homogenized pro football that the NFL wants to sell you. You'll definitely see coaches, players, and fans in the throes of passion, saying and doing things they would never otherwise think of. The linemen who love contact—they're trying to rip somebody's head off! It's all part of our reality show, the one no one else would have the balls to do.

While McMahon wasn't quite such a braggart following the first few weeks of the season, there's a good chance he felt like a 12-foot penis. And if he didn't, he should have. Though the XFL was able to score a huge 9.5 rating for its debut, the hype soon wore off and was replaced by the realization that the football itself was not very good. I take that back — it wasn't just "not very good," it was very not good. A lot of that had to do to the fact that teams were given very little time to practice together. Apparently, little thought was given to the actual games themselves, with

ANDRE J. BEAUCAGE

The XFL started with a bang, which no doubt made Vince McMahon downright giddy. He probably wasn't quite so happy a few weeks later when the games drew the lowest ratings in television history.

the belief that the wild nature of the rules would cover up any deficiencies the teams themselves might have. This line of thinking, however, ignored the fact that the rules themselves weren't really all that different from those of the league the XFL was mocking.

For example, it was declared that the "fair catch" rule in the NFL was for wimps. Announcers repeatedly harped about how there would be no fair catches in the XFL. Imagine the surprise during the first punt of the season when the man downfield caught the ball and his opponents stood around watching him without making contact. Sure, there wasn't a fair catch, but there was a "halo" of five yards. There were all kinds of little sub-rules like this to cover up the fact that, yes, this was just like the NFL, no matter how the announcers attempted to spin it. Well, actually, there was one major difference between the two leagues: the XFL players were now-here near as good.

McMahon and his crew tried everything to salvage the league. Commentator Jesse Ventura had ragged on New York/New Jersey Hitmen coach Rusty Tillman during the first game of the season, so McMahon, seeing this as an opportunity to "create controversy," egged him on. A thrilling rivalry followed, as Ventura called Tillman "gutless" at every opportunity. Tillman did what anyone other than a pro wrestler would do — he ignored him. Although the league was desperate to stir the pot, Tillman wanted no part of it, and refused to play along.

The league was becoming a very uncool thing to be associated with, so more drastic measures were taken. As part of what they acknowledged to be a "cheap publicity stunt," the league promised to go inside the cheer-leader's locker room. This time, though, fans knew better. And, sure enough, there were no hot chicks showering. Instead, viewers were treated to a corn-ball dream sequence after hapless cameraman Bruno hit his head against a wall. The segment featured girls playing Twister with men dressed up as gorillas. It was like *Girls Gone Wild* Meets *Planet of the Apes*, except with a decided lack of nudity. The bit ended with McMahon himself waking Bruno from his slumber.

McMahon had gone into the venture with grand dreams of record ratings. And that's just what he got. Ratings for games near the end of the season dropped to 1.5, which is the all-time lowest rating ever for a prime-time network program. Every other show in the entire history of prime-time television scored a higher rating. *Every single show ever.* Remember *Hello, Larry*, the late-'70s sitcom starring McLean Stevenson as a disc jockey? Of course you don't. No one does. But that doesn't change the fact that it was a more popular program than the XFL broadcasts.

This was the WBF all over again, just on a much larger scale. But it wasn't McMahon's fault, of course. McMahon attempted to spin things the other direction via an interview for HBO's *On the Record with Bob Costas*. During the interview, he claimed that the reason the league was failing was due to the fact that the "elitist" media, such as Costas, weren't taking it seriously. It was the biased media, who always were and always would be against him and anything he tried. That's all it was. They never covered the league. They never gave it a chance. Folks at home dismissed it because it was being ridiculed. It wasn't the football, and it wasn't anything McMahon had done wrong. It was the media that killed the XFL. Nothing else.

Despite the abject failure of the XFL, Vince still had the WWF to fall back on, and that was certainly good enough. After all, wrestling, not football, had made him a billionaire. And while some would say that the WWF's fortunes had turned largely due to the hard work of men such as Steve Austin and the Rock, McMahon knew there was more to it than that. There was no way either man would have achieved such greatness without his vision. He had created both characters. No one else could have done it. After all, Eric Bischoff, the whiz kid who led WCW to new heights, had said that Austin would never draw. In fact, Bischoff had fired Austin from WCW for just that reason.

And where was Bischoff now? Nowhere. Bischoff was nowhere because he didn't have the foresight that Vince had. He wasn't as smart as Vince.

He didn't promote a show as good as the WWF's. And now he was gone, just like all those other old-time promoters Vince had sent packing years earlier. See you later, Eric. You will never, ever be on a wrestling show again.

Yes, this was sweet. But even McMahon could never have dreamed just how wonderfully sweet it would become. On March 26, 2001, the final night of the Monday Night Wars, McMahon would bestow the ultimate embarrassment on his old foe Ted Turner. For he, Vince McMahon, would open the final *Nitro* with a live simulcast from the *Raw* show in Cleveland. And he would do it on Turner's very own network:

Imagine that. Me. Vince McMahon. Imagine that! Here I am on WCW television. How can that happen? Well there's only one way. You see, it was just a matter of time before I, Vince McMahon, bought my competition. That's right! I *own* WCW! Therefore, in its final broadcast tonight on TNT, I have the opportunity to address you, the WCW fans. I have an opportunity to address you, the WCW superstars. What is the fate of WCW? Well, tonight, in a special simulcast, you'll all find out, because the very fate of WCW is in *my* hands.

It was a speech that he had no doubt wanted to give since the Billionaire Ted days, and now he was not only giving it to Turner, but he was doing so on Turner's own dime. Screw you, Ted Turner. Screw you.

After the final match of the evening, pitting longtime rivals Ric Flair and Sting against each other one last time, McMahon appeared again on-screen to those watching live in Panama City and to those glued to their sets on both TNN and TNT. He began to run down WCW and its talent, going so far as to poll fans in attendance as to whom he should keep. This was the ultimate ego trip: he was virtually firing those who had deserted him years earlier live on national TV.

Suddenly, Vince's son Shane appeared live in the WCW ring in Panama City. He explained that he, not Vince, had bought WCW and they were about to kick the WWF's ass all over again. (This was, of course, all part of the story line.) Shane then reiterated that he would be facing Vince at *Wrestlemania* later in the week. The final segment of wrestling on a Turner network that had carried WCW for almost 20 years was a WWF *Wrestlemania X7* commercial.

It should be noted that while the final *Nitro* was dubbed the "Night of Champions," it was anything but. Vince may have ranted and raved about firing Hogan, Goldberg, Nash, and others, but in reality none of those guys were even at the final broadcast. The company had destroyed so many working relationships that these men, along with countless others, simply decided to forgo appearing on the show that they had helped build. In their place were men like Kid Romeo and "Sugar" Shane Helms. Talented guys, certainly, but in terms of name recognition they were nobodies.

That was where McMahon would come in. If there was one thing Vince was good at, it was turning nobodies into somebodies. He had something else now, too: the WCW name. Despite the fact that the promotion had gone in the toilet, the name could still boost Vince's fortunes if he played his cards right. For years, every wrestling fan in the country wanted to see WCW vs. the WWF. And now he could present it, without fear of a lawsuit, because he owned everything. It was as though he had just been handed the keys to Fort Knox and told to take whatever he wanted.

At *Wrestlemania X7*, Shane beat Vince as the WCW crew looked on. However, they weren't ringside, or backstage. Instead, they were in the rafters, and no one was even identified by name. This certainly wasn't a very impressive debut for a group that was to be the focal point of an interpromotional feud the likes of which the business had never seen. Still, it was understandable; the deal to purchase WCW was completed literally the week before *Wrestlemania,* and therefore the company hadn't had time to properly plan ahead.

Over the course of the next several months, WCW wrestlers Diamond Dallas Page, Booker T, and others began popping up and attacking WWF stars. This would have made for great television, but as had often happened in WCW, backstage politics got in the way. Behind the scenes, wrestlers who had been in the WWF since before the so-called invasion were concerned that the newcomers might take their spots on the roster. This led to several WWF stars concocting stories about how the WCW crew was clumsy and dangerous to work with in the ring.

Vince not only bought into the story, but he also went one step further. He began to believe that these WCW workers were completely inferior to his WWF superstars. Therefore, WWF guys were instructed to defeat the newcomers at every opportunity. More often than not, the WWF crew didn't simply beat WCW, they humiliated them.

Case in point: Diamond Dallas Page debuted by stalking the Undertaker's wife, Sarah. As he was one of the first WCW invaders, the arena came unglued upon his arrival, and ratings nudged upward. This should have led to a hard-fought feud in which Page got the early upper hand, with Undertaker avenging his wife at the end.

That's not what happened. Instead, Undertaker absolutely murdered Page in each and every match. Rare was the occasion when DDP got in even one offensive move. Just to make sure Page and the rest of WCW looked like complete losers, Sarah, who had never even been seen on WWF TV before and had zero training, beat DDP as well!

This, along with Team WCW being punked out by WWF midcarders, led fans to believe that WCW didn't have a chance in the feud. That led to falling ratings, which Vince attributed to the WCW guys simply not being able to draw. Of course, since it was Vince who had put them in that position by killing them week after week, you'd think he might have shouldered some of the blame.

But having read this far into the book, you certainly know better than that.

Keep in mind that Vince owned WCW. Had he positioned the WCW group as a legitimate threat, there would have been an insane amount of money to be made. Remember that the best way to make money in wrestling is to give fans the illusion that either side could win. That never happened, because Vince didn't want the WWF to look bad, even momentarily, against his "old rival." Of course, WCW wasn't even a rival, since he now owned them!

In an attempt to salvage the situation, Extreme Championship Wrestling was added to the mix. ECW was a wild organization based out of Philadelphia that featured hard-hitting action with wild story lines. With Heyman under contract, an ECW invasion was devised to help boost sagging ratings. This, too, was a failure, but for a completely different reason from the WCW fiasco. With the lone exceptions of Rob Van Dam and Tommy Dreamer, the ECW force was comprised of men such as the Dudley Boyz and Tazz, who had been working for the WWF for quite some time.

Sure, these men had competed in ECW at some point in their careers, but they had worked for the WWF just as long, and in some cases, longer. Therefore, the matches that were presented were exactly the same as the ones the WWF had been presenting for years. Fans didn't buy them "jumping sides" because they had already seen the exact same men paired off against the WWF crew countless times. The Hardy Boyz vs. Dudley Boyz matches were exactly the same as before, the only difference being that now the fans were supposed to suddenly believe that the Dudleyz were with ECW. And fans were tired of that match, no matter how the teams were aligned.

Still believing they could rectify the situation, they created yet another angle in which WCW and ECW formed an alliance under the guidance of Shane and Stephanie McMahon. And that was really the death of the entire invasion story line, as the focus shifted away from WCW and ECW vs. the WWF and back to the McMahons, none of whom were even wrestlers!

It was understandable that Vince and his family had been originally recruited to be on the air. During the period in which WCW was scooping up WWF talent at will, Vince knew that although everyone else in the company was potentially up for grabs, his family would remain. Therefore, the four immediate family members were given on-screen roles.

Linda, Vince's wife, appeared frequently to chastise Vince for his evil actions. This set up some unique interaction, although Linda herself would admit she was somewhere between a walnut and an oak on the acting-ability scale. Still, this didn't keep the company from trotting her out occasionally. One such angle saw Vince driving Linda insane and locking her up in an institution. Perhaps he had found Teddy Long's big gold key.

To ensure that his evil plans wouldn't be foiled, Vince paid off the staff at the asylum to keep Linda drugged. About this time, he began cavorting with a 25-year-old blond bombshell by the name of Trish Stratus. A truly tasteful segment had Vince and Trish making out as the doped-up Linda looked on. Linda must legitimately be a very understanding woman to watch her real-life husband mack on a woman half his age right in front of her. And Vince must be a really depraved individual for doing so.

Shane was the stuntman of the family. Not only would he get into the ring and square off against WWF wrestlers, but he would also attempt to steal the show at every opportunity by taking insane risks. If he wasn't dropping elbows from 30 feet off the ground, he was being thrown through plate glass windows. Although he is an asset in the ring, he seemingly feels that he can contribute more to the company by putting his Boston University communications degree to work as director of new media, handling the company's Internet presence and working on television production, than by stepping back into the ring. Therefore, his time on television over the past few years has diminished.

Which is far from the case with his sister, Stephanie, the biggest camera hog since the old man himself. Stephanie first appeared on WWF TV as an angelic little girl who fell in love with former Mötley Crüe bodyguard Andrew "Test" Martin. The two were set to be wed on WWF TV, when the nefarious Triple H interrupted the ceremony, claiming that he had already married Steph at a drive-through wedding chapel in Las Vegas. Sure enough, he produced footage of himself and Stephanie exchanging their vows. The catch was that Stephanie had been knocked out, so Hunter did a bad ventriloquist act for her "I dos." Eventually, she aligned herself with Hunter, turned on her family, and got herself a big balloony boob job in the process.

Behind the scenes, things were even more interesting. Stephanie and Hunter became a real-life couple, driving Triple H's former girlfriend Chyna from the promotion and into a life of B movies and car show appearances. Vince also gave Steph the reins as head of the creative staff, which led to Hunter being pushed to the moon and more Stephanie on screen than the fans ever wanted. It was all Steph and all Hunter, all the time!

Despite the fact that there were at least a half-dozen more attractive women in the promotion, feuds suddenly revolved around men fighting over Stephanie. One such feud played out over months and months and featured Kurt Angle attempting to woo Stephanie away from Hunter. Angle would sneak a kiss in here and there when Hunter wasn't around, playing the smarmy, girlfriend-stealing-heel role to the hilt. As the feud built to its zenith, it was clear what the fans wanted: Steph to go with Angle, turning Hunter babyface in the process.

The problem was that behind the scenes, Hunter didn't want to turn face, and he certainly didn't want his real-life girlfriend hanging out with the most over heel in the company. Therefore, the expected swerve — Stephanie turning on Hunter — never came about. The feud simply fizzled out, and Hunter and Steph remained together, despite the fact that this wasn't what the fans wanted to see. It didn't matter what the fans wanted; what mattered was what Hunter and Steph wanted. This turned off an enormous chunk of the fan base, especially the females at whom the story line had been targeted. Surely, there should have been some sort of payoff.

Eventually, Steph and Hunter did break up as an on-screen couple, but Kurt wasn't involved at all. Those who thought this would actually improve the situation were sorely disappointed when the breakup finally went down. While they were no longer hogging the spotlight together, the side effect of the two parting ways was that now they could be in twice as many segments. Yay!

Because they occupied so much valuable television time, others within the promotion were seriously shortchanged. Take, for example, Chris Jericho. After being buried for most of his WWF career, Jericho was given a shot at the top of the promotion. Fans had been calling for this since his debut with the company, but those backstage continually undermined any progress he made (read: Hunter didn't like him). He was finally put over Steve Austin and the Rock in the same night to become the first-ever

"Undisputed" Champion, merging the WWF and WCW title belts. Of course, since the WCW Invasion had been such a bust, the WCW title didn't mean much anymore. Still, beating Austin and Rock was nothing to sneeze at.

As *Wrestlemania X8* approached, Hunter came back from an injury and was immediately positioned to headline the biggest pay-per-view of the year in a title match with Jericho. Of course, Stephanie also had to be involved, so she became Jericho's manager, despite the fact that Jericho had called her a "low-life, bottom-feeding, trashbag ho" every time the two shared a stage since her arrival in the promotion. It didn't matter that it made no sense; what mattered is that Stephanie was once again involved in the main-event story line heading into the biggest show of the year. As time went on, the spotlight continued to fade from Jericho and focus more tightly on the domestic squabbles of Hunter and Steph. Even their dog, a mangy mutt by the name of Lucy, got screen time. By the time the title match rolled around, Jericho was reduced to cleaning up after Lucy.

Think about that. The world champion of the promotion was not only playing second fiddle to the head writer and her boyfriend, but he was also being forced to pick up their dog's crap. To almost no one's surprise, the ratings and buy rates continued their downward spiral. And who got the blame? It wasn't Hunter. And it sure as hell wasn't Stephanie — she was a McMahon, after all. It wasn't even Lucy. It was, of course, Chris Jericho, because he supposedly didn't know how to work and because fans didn't take him seriously.

One demonstration of just how desperate Vince had become by this time over the ratings free-fall was his decision to bring back three men who no one ever thought would be seen again in a WWF ring: Scott Hall, Kevin Nash, and Hulk Hogan.

Unbelievably, McMahon brought in the nWo.

To say that this was a disaster would be a huge understatement. Scott Hall was way past the point of being useful as an in-ring competitor. His "personal demons," which had led to his demise in WCW, were once again becoming a problem, as he would often show up to events in no condition to perform. Nash was also in no condition to perform, but that was more due to the fact that his body was becoming more and more brittle with each passing day. During one of his first matches for the WWF, he injured his bicep. After taking several months off to allow it to heal, he came back and in his very first match, he tore his quadriceps while simply walking across the ring, putting himself out of action for over a year!

This left an ancient Hulk Hogan to carry the group, which was problematic as well. For while Hogan was, ironically, the healthiest of the three, a large portion of the WWF fan base still viewed him as an icon, and therefore cheered his every move. This catapulted to Hogan to the WWF title yet again, which was good in the short term. However, nostalgia dies off quickly, and so did the ratings and buy rates. For his part, though, Hogan wasn't the political nightmare he had been in WCW, and he now did what was asked of him, even allowing rookie sensation Brock Lesnar to put him on the shelf.

By far the biggest problem with the WWF version of the nWo was that unlike in WCW, where they were allowed to run roughshod over the entire promotion, this incarnation was never portrayed as anything more than a hapless group of thugs. It was the WCW invasion all over again, just with higher-priced talent whose bodies were falling apart.

No one wanted to work with them. Steve Austin, in particular, had little desire to even get into the ring with the nWo, let alone put them over. He specifically did not want to work with Scott Hall. Austin's fear was that

Hall might once again show up drun — —. . . er . . . that is, "confronting his personal demons." Austin believed this would increase the odds of Hall not taking proper care to ensure the safety of his neck, which had been fragile since a freak accident in a match with Owen Hart in 1997. Austin therefore refused to be the patsy in this feud, which nullified the nWo as a legitimate threat. Within weeks, Hall was fired, Nash was injured, and Hogan was on his nostalgia run.

Austin was sick of the whole scene. He was tired of the lack of focus the promotion had, and what he dubbed the "piss poor" writing of Stephanie and her crew. More than anything, however, he was sick of Hunter and Steph being the focus of the promotion that he had brought to greatness. Knowing that changes were not forthcoming, Austin simply walked off the set. He left not only the WWF, but the industry as well, for even if he had been able to get out of his contract (and make no mistake about it, McMahon wouldn't have released Austin in a million years), there was nowhere else to go. That's how frustrated he was with the situation: he was willing to retire rather than deal with the headaches the McMahons were creating on a daily basis due to nepotism and a total lack of understanding of the business.

Vince was furious at Austin's behavior and buried him over and over again on WWF TV. He spoke of how the WWF made Austin a star, and how "Stone Cold" was just a baby who took his ball and went home. Jim Ross compared Austin leaving to John Wayne being a coward, although if Wayne were ever forced to take direction from Stephanie with her fingernails-on-chalkboard voice, he'd probably have ridden off into the sunset too.

Things were rapidly spinning out of control for the WWF when they were hit by yet another disaster. The World Wildlife Fund, which had been battling McMahon for years over the rights to the initials WWF, had finally prevailed in a court battle in the United Kingdom. This had been brewing for quite some time, as the wrestling company had lost a legal battle in 1994, which led to an agreement between the two groups that limited the wrestling promotion's use of the initials. McMahon basically crossed his heart and hoped to die and promised he would never do that again. He must have had his fingers crossed behind his back, because he went right on using the WWF name.

In May of 2002, England's House of Lords forced McMahon's hand, and the wrestling company was required to change its name. The company responded by dropping the "Federation" moniker and adding an E for entertainment. The new name was World Wrestling Entertainment, which everyone from fans to those within the company absolutely hated. They were also forced to change their website address, which was one of the most popular in the world. Of course, had McMahon simply offered to donate a million or so a year to the Wildlife Fund, odds are this could have all been avoided. But then, that wouldn't have been the McMahon way.

No, the McMahon way was to do business as it had always been done, and if something had worked in the past, it would work in today's market as well. The most shocking incident of the year may have been this brief announcement on the newly christened wwe.com on June 20, 2002: "World Wrestling Entertainment welcomes back Vince Russo to the creative writing team."

Yes, Vince Russo. The man who had destroyed WCW was not only back with WWE, but he was also given almost full control of the creative aspect of the company. Vince McMahon felt that Russo's outlandish nature could be of value to the struggling creative department. Online fans, who had come to know Russo during his WCW tenure, were shocked. So was the WWE creative team, which nearly mutinied upon hearing the news. McMahon realized that he couldn't go on with just Russo, so he relented and sent him packing.

That the idea was even given thought was scary enough. What may have been even more frightening was the fact that the McMahons seemingly had no clue how to stop the bleeding. Therefore, much as WCW had done, WWE simply began bringing back every "name" they could find in an effort to enhance ratings. Scott Steiner, who had been diagnosed with drop foot syndrome, a condition in which the victim has a hard time controlling movement in his feet, was brought in and immediately pushed into a feud with Triple H. This resulted in one of the worst matches ever on pay-per-view. At *Royal Rumble 2003*, Steiner blew move after move, prompting the crowd to nearly boo him out of the building. This despite the fact that he was a babyface! At one point, his cardiovascular conditioning was so bad that he collapsed into the ropes, with many fearing he had suffered a heart attack. Still, since he was big and muscular and looked the part, he was given a rematch at *No Way Out*.

And what was that a few pages ago about Eric Bischoff? Let's go back and check: "And where was Bischoff now? Nowhere. Bischoff was nowhere because he didn't have the foresight that Vince had. He wasn't as smart as Vince. He didn't promote a show as good as the WWF's. And now he was gone, just like all those other old-time promoters Vince had sent packing years earlier. See you later, Eric. You will never, ever be on a wrestling show again."

On July 15, 2002, Eric Bischoff made his WWE debut on *Raw*, live from New Jersey. As part of the story line, McMahon named him the general manager of *Raw* then gave him a big hug and left the arena.

Now if you've read this far into the book, you will remember that Vince McMahon and Eric Bischoff legitimately hated each other. In wrestling, however, the opportunity to make money overrides such petty emotions, so the hiring of Bischoff, while truly a shocking occurrence, was not as astonishing as the fact that he was aligned on-screen with Vince McMahon.

McMahon and Bischoff did hate each other. Fans knew it. Many fans didn't consider the WCW and nWo invasions of the WWF to be legitimate simply because Bischoff wasn't there. That's how closely identified he was with the factions. Bringing in Bischoff was the one last, legitimate shot at having an invasion angle work because of the built-in animosity of the men involved. Fans would believe Bischoff as an invader because there was no one who had ever professed as much hatred for Vince McMahon.

Therefore, when McMahon and Bischoff hugged, they flushed away millions upon millions of dollars. Bischoff was essentially given McMahon's old role of evil company owner, a part that fans had long tired of, no matter who was wearing the suit. It made zero sense.

Of course, since Bischoff was controlling *Raw*, there needed to be a GM on the company's *SmackDown* program as well. Let's see . . . whom could we put in a role that requires no actual wrestling ability but involves inordinate amounts of screen time? I know! How about Stephanie McMahon? The last thing fans wanted was more Stephanie, but since her daddy had given her control, that's exactly what they got. To the shock of no one except those with the surname of McMahon, ratings started dropping to levels they hadn't reached since before *Nitro* was launched.

McMahon, seeing his crowds dwindling, theorized that what had brought them to the top of the mountain was outlandish raunch. He therefore advised his creative crew to come up with more sexual, soap opera story lines. By returning to the raunchy style of old, they would force the media to cover WWE as they had before the bottom started falling out.

With this in mind, the gay tag team of Billy and Chuck was created. The team, comprised of former DX member Billy Gunn and WCW outcast Chuck Palumbo, gave each other gifts, like matching headbands and trunks. They also had a penchant for helping each other stretch out before the matches in a vaguely homosexual manner.

They were prime candidates for wrestling's first-ever gay wedding. WWE went full bore with the promotion of the event, which landed them the mainstream coverage they so desired. The *New York Times*, the *Washington Post*, and even *The Today Show* mentioned the event. This was what McMahon had wanted. Everything was set for the nuptials to take place on the September 12, 2002 edition of *SmackDown*.

Not that there was ever really a plan to have the two wed. On that fateful night, as they stood in the center of the ring to be married, Billy and Chuck balked at the last minute, claiming they were both straight. This was simply a publicity stunt that had gone way, way too far, they explained. (Rest assured that this was all part of the story line and was discussed beforehand.) The ceremony ended with Eric Bischoff and his hit squad attacking the groom and . . . groom, leaving them facedown on the mat.

This infuriated such groups as the Gay and Lesbian Alliance Against Defamation (GLAAD), which had initially supported the event, and therefore helped WWE to get the mainstream publicity they were looking for. Heck, they even gave Billy and Chuck a wedding gift (a gravy boat from the Pottery Barn) on the *The Today Show*!

"The WWE lied to us two months ago when they promised that Billy and Chuck would come out and wed on the air," fumed GLAAD spokesman Scott Seomin in a press release following the event. "In fact, I was told (lied to) the day after the show was taped in Minneapolis that the wedding took place and all was well."

But McMahon didn't care. So they had lied to a few folks. So what? This was the wrestling business, and lying was what the business was built upon. Besides, wrestling was once again in the news, and that's all he really cared about. If this gay wedding stunt could get them this much publicity, imagine what more outlandish events could do. McMahon ordered his crew to come up with more such "life events" for WWE TV. More weddings, birthday parties—heck, throw in a bar mitzvah if you want! And most of all, more sex!

All manner of sexual deviant was brought to the ring. Strippers were brought out to perform "Hot Lesbian Action" before live crowds, which involved exchanging kisses while wearing underwear. Probably not as "hot" as most people were expecting, but as much as the networks would allow. WWE were so pleased with this stunt that they designed an HLA T-shirt, complete with a logo of a tongue, a plus sign, and a cardboard box. No one bought it.

In another story line, a 65-year-old man was married to a twenty-something brunette beauty while wearing nothing more than his under-pants. The old man later "died" while on his honeymoon. The cause? Too much sex, of course.

There was just one thing these angles were missing, though, and McMahon knew exactly what it was: necrophilia. "When he came up with the idea, it was all he could talk about," claimed a former WWE employee who requested anonymity. "He just kept yelling out the punchline to the skit then laughing uncontrollably. It was very uncomfortable."

The angle came about because Triple H was having a problem finding credible opponents. It wasn't so much the case that they couldn't find opponents, but rather that he and Steph were having a tough time finding opponents who wouldn't overshadow him. They therefore allowed Kane, a character who had been floating in the midcard for years, to become the top contender to Hunter's title. However, since Kane had done nothing of note to explain his number-one contendership, a story line was concocted that would push him up the rankings.

Hunter accused Kane of murdering his (Kane's) high school sweetheart, Katie Vick. Since the words "Katie Vick" had never been muttered on WWE television before, fans had no idea who Hunter was talking about. An elaborate back story was created in which Kane and cheerleader Katie were friends who had been out at a party late one rainy evening some ten years before. Kane claimed he was unfamiliar with a stick shift, which caused him to swerve off the road and ram into a tree, killing Katie instantly. Hunter didn't believe this, claiming that Kane had intentionally killed Katie after she had spurned one of his sexual advances. It got much worse, as Hunter alleged that during the autopsy the coroner had discovered traces of Kane's semen in Katie's body. Hunter continued needling Kane, asking, "On that night, did you force Katie Vick to have sex with you while she was alive, or did you wait and do it to her after she was dead?"

All this would have been disgusting enough, but Hunter went further, producing footage of the night Kane did the dirty deed. A videotape, with the date "10/09/92" in the corner, displayed a casket decorated with pom-poms and flowers. Quietly, a familiar figure entered the room.

It was Kane; or rather, it was Hunter disguised as Kane. He began talking to Katie (actually a mannequin) as though she were still alive, which would have been creepy enough. However, he began to "hear" her, and she was making it very clear that she wanted him. She wanted him in a *sexual* manner. The shot pixilated as he groped her breasts then pulled off her panties, stopping to take a whiff. He then stripped buck nekked, hopped in the casket, spread her legs, and banged her gong. Following this, he proclaimed some weird type of carnal victory, screaming, "I did it, I really did it! I screwed your brains out!" He then grabbed a fistful of noodles and threw them at the screen.

Somewhere, Vince McMahon was no doubt laughing his head off.

While McMahon found all this humorous, fans didn't. And the media, which had flocked to the gay wedding just weeks before, didn't even make mention of it. The ratings for the following week's show completely collapsed, as fans tuned out in droves. They had seen enough, and they didn't want to stick around for the encore (which involved Hunter doing a ventriloquist bit with Katie, whom he wheeled out in a casket).

McMahon didn't understand. This was far more outrageous than the gay wedding. Why didn't the media cover it? Why were fans leaving? And what could he do to keep his rapidly diminishing fan base tuning in?

After all McMahon and his WWF/WWE had been through, it was unfathomable that they were losing their audience so quickly. He had run WCW out of business. He had created star after star. He had sold out arenas and made himself a billionaire. He had done it all. He was Vince McMahon, damn it!

Ironically enough, despite all his wealth and all his fame and all his vast knowledge of the business, McMahon was right back where he started: throwing whatever he could think up against the wall to see what would stick.

And though WWE will almost certainly rebound from its funk, in the meantime it appears that all Vince has left to throw against the wall is crap.

WrestleCrap, that is.

Sources

Berardinelli, James. ReelViews.

   http://moviereviews.colossus.net/movies/m/mr_nanny.html.

Ebert, Roger, "*Commando* Might Entertain Hulk Hogan Fans," *Chicago Sun-Times*, 4 October 1991, sec. Weekend Plus, p.48.

Home Team Sportsbeat. 30 June 1986.

Oliver, Greg. Slam Wrestling Web site.

   www.canoe.ca/SlamWrestlingBios/shaw_mike.html.

Warrior. Scottsdale, AZ: Ultimate Creations, 1996.